Some Dark Fire

ALSO BY MICHAEL LIEBERMAN

POETRY

Praising with My Body

A History of the Sweetness of the World

Sojourn at Elmhurst, A Poem Sequence

Remnant

Far-From-Equilibrium Conditions

Bonfire of the Verities

The Houstiliad, An Iliad *for Houston*

FICTION

Never Surrender — Never Retreat, A Novel of Medical Politics in Texas

The Lobsterman's Daughter

The Women of Harvard Square, A Novel in Short Stories

Some Dark Fire

New and Selected Poems
(1992 – 2016)

Michael Lieberman

TEXAS REVIEW PRESS
HUNTSVILLE, TEXAS

FIRST EDITION

Requests for permission to acknowledge material from this work should be sent to:

Permissions
Texas Review Press
English Department
Sam Houston State University
Huntsville, TX 77341-2146

To learn more about Michael Lieberman and his work or to contact him:

website: michaellieberman.com
email: poet@lieberman.net

Acknowledgements:
With the exception of the new poems in "Views of Eden," the poems in this volume are drawn from books published by: New Rivers Press (Minneapolis, now in Moorhead, MN), Sheep Meadow Press (New York, NY), Texas Review Press (Huntsville, TX), and Thorn Books (Houston, TX). My gratitude to individual poets and friends is profound and expressed in the introductory essay, "Art is a Debtor's Prison." The dedication of this book to my wife Susan doesn't begin to express my limitless debt to a remarkable woman and my love as well. Profound thanks are due Dr. Paul Ruffin, Editor-in-Chief of Texas Review Press—he was a good friend and steadfast supporter. I will miss him. Rich Levy, Dave Parsons, Don Schofield, and Sandi Stromberg have read some of my recent work and provided thoughtful comments. Thanks to all of you. I am indebted, as always, to Nancy Parsons for a fine cover. It is a pleasure to work with someone so intuitive and smart about melding the visual with the written. Thanks to Kim Davis of Texas Review Press, who so carefully and painstakingly formatted and edited this book. Thanks also to Julian Kindred and Catherine Smith who helped proofread.

Cover Design by Nancy Parsons

Library of Congress Cataloging-in-Publication Data

Names: Lieberman, Michael, 1941- author.
Title: Some dark fire : new and selected poems (1992-2016) / Michael
    Lieberman.
Description: First edition. | Huntsville, Texas : Texas Review Press, [2016]
    | Previously-published material, with the exception of the introductory
    essay (Art is a debtor's prison) and the first collection of poems (Views
    of Eden). | Includes bibliographical references.
Identifiers: LCCN 2016032140 (print) | LCCN 2016033043 (ebook) | ISBN
    9781680031072 (hardback) | ISBN 9781680031089 (e-book) | ISBN
    9781680031089 (ebook)
Subjects: | LCGFT: Poetry
Classification: LCC PS3562.I434 A6 2016 (print) | LCC PS3562.I434 (ebook) |
    DDC 811/.54--dc23
LC record available at https://lccn.loc.gov/2016032140

Dedication

for Susan,
there can be no other

In Memory of

Paul Ruffin (1941-2016)

Contents

from *Sojourn at Elmhurst, A Poem Sequence* (1998)

from *Remnant* (2002)

from *Far-From-Equilibrium Conditions* (2007)

Art is a Debtor's Prison

I'm sitting on Jack's living room floor in the Robert Francis House in Amherst, my poems scattered everywhere—and suffering from a paralysis of good fortune. I had driven down the night before from a scientific meeting in New Hampshire to spend a few days with Jack Gilbert and Linda Gregg. Jack is a hard ass when it comes to poetry. And a night on his couch confirms this judgment. I am stiff and grumpy.

Coffee in hand, I look at Jack, who seems to have slept just fine. Thorn Books, a small Houston press, wants to bring out my chapbook, I tell him, and I have no idea which poems to include or how to order them. An enviable problem, and I know it. Victor Espino has heard me read at an open mic at the Old Firehouse on Westheimer in Houston. On the spot, he has offered to publish a book—an utterly astounding gift, a one in a million occurrence. That was in the late winter of 1992. Now it's June, and I'm stuck.

Let me say in fulsome voice: I am one lucky son of a bitch. Art is a debtor's prison, and I have been sentenced to life.

What's it called? *Praising with My Body*, I say. Jack looks interested. And the problem? I reiterate my dilemma. Let me have a look, and we gather the poems. What happens next can only be described as miraculous. Almost as fast as he can shuffle, he discards the weaker poems and orders the rest. I change nothing. This is the manuscript I give to Victor when I return to Houston.

Jack, I say sheepishly, I have another problem. You've put my poems about Aphrodite in the center of the book. What's a fifty-one year old physician doing writing poems about Aphrodite? Jack is dismayed. He shoots me a look— the exasperated look we reserve for hopeless cases. What else would one write poems about?

Other debts. The backstory: I had started writing poems again in Philadelphia after a twenty-year hiatus. A few years later in 1988 we moved to Houston, and my friend Milt

MacLeod put me in touch with Ed Hirsch, then at the University of Houston (UH). Ed very kindly looked at some of my poems. The graduate writing seminars at UH were open only to fulltime graduate students, he explained. But I should apply to the Squaw Valley Community of Writers poetry workshop. If they take you, you should go. They took me, and there on two separate occasions I worked with Galway Kinnell, Sharon Olds, Bob Hass, and other fine poets. It's really where I learned to write a poem that others might want to read. It was their no nonsense, no bullshit tough love that freed me up. It's been a long road, but it was there that I began to learn how to get out of my head and write from my heart and my unconscious

Don Schofield, a poet I met at Squaw, mentioned that Linda Gregg, whose poetry he loved, was teaching an undergraduate workshop in the fall at the UH, and I might want to sit in. I audited the course, wrote a lot of bad poems, and developed a friendship. What followed was long-distance mentoring by Linda and Jack. I would call them in New York. One would get on the line, and I would read a poem. Then the other got on, and I read it again. I held my breath: I don't think you're there yet. That's not really a poem. You can do better. I don't get it. The thing has no heart. Finally months later Jack said, That's a poem. So when I showed up in Amherst and wizard Jack organized my poems with lightning speed, he had a bit of a leg up from his telecounseling. Still, I remain amazed at his deft intelligence.

With a little confidence and *Praising with My Body* on the shelf, I put together a full-length manuscript and sent it off — along with twenty bucks a pop — to first book contests. Surprise, surprise, the world didn't love my poetry as much as I thought it should. You have to have a thick skin or a taste for masochism to be a poet. Then luck struck again. Walt McDonald, a fine West Texas poet, selected my manuscript from what must have been a daunting stack of "blind" submissions for a first book contest, run by Texas Review Press at Sam Houston State University. And in 1995 Paul Ruffin, the director/editor-in-chief of the press, brought out *A History of the Sweetness of the World*. In Paul, I found a friend and ardent supporter of my work.

Somehow in the early to mid nineties I met Adam Zagajewski, who was then teaching a graduate European literature seminar each year at the UH. While the writing workshops were off-limits, auditing the literature seminar was not, or at least not as far as Adam was concerned. I spent half a dozen years reading and learning — and developing a friendship. It's hard to imagine my poems without this experience. The ancients and moderns, almost always from continental Europe, were added to my narrow list of Chaucer to Eliot and Auden and contemporary American voices. How else would I have found Aleksander Wat or Gottfried Benn? And through Adam I came to love Zbigniew Herbert.

In 1998 New Rivers Press, then in Minneapolis, published *Sojourn at Elmhurst*. It was a radical departure, a poem sequence that told the story of Frank Goldin, a middle-aged biochemist, who commits himself to Elmhurst, a psychiatric hospital. I had never before written so many poems around a theme. It remains some of my best work and served, I think, as an unconscious model for *The Houstiliad, An* Iliad *for Houston*, my most recent book. That story imagines Achilles and many of Homer's other characters alive in contemporary Houston. No one reads book-length poems in the twenty-first century, and *The Houstiliad* owes its publication to Paul Ruffin's faith in me as a poet.

Luck struck again in 2002 when I showed a collection of Holocaust poems to my friend Dan Stern, then the Cullen Professor of Literature at UH, and now sadly deceased. He liked them and called his friend, the poet Stanley Moss, director of Sheep Meadow Press. Would he be willing to read an unsolicited manuscript? Stanley too liked the poems, and in three days it was settled. Sheep Meadow would publish my poems. Only it wasn't settled, not at all. Stanley was a very demanding editor and forced me to write and rewrite and rewrite my poems until I had a much better book. The result was *Remnant*. Stanley was a stern warder, but I was fortunate that he jailed me.

Since then I have worked closely with Paul and Texas Review Press, which brought out *Far-From-Equilibrium Conditions* (2007), *Bonfire of the Verities* (2013), *The Houstiliad, an* Iliad *for Houston* (2015), and the present volume. I have been far luckier than most poets.

Among writers, poets especially crave readers. It's only a slight exaggeration to say that people don't read poetry today unless they write it. Regardless of W.C. Williams' warning that

". . . men die miserably every day / for lack / of what is found there," we get our news and our sustenance from the Internet, our mobile devices, a few news networks, perhaps a newspaper (often online), and less commonly novels or nonfiction. Poets remember the good old days. Really? The good old days when Keats' publisher brought out his first book in an edition of 200 and couldn't give them away; when Whitman self-published the first edition of *Leaves of Grass,* and Dickinson saw only a handful of her poems published in her lifetime. And we non-luminaries, let me call us 3-watt wonders — night-light poets — how about us? Well, we hardly exist. And I for one feel lucky. I have some supportive readers, but mostly I'm left alone. Which frees me. I don't have the expectations of other people warping my instincts. I can change subject or focus or style without facing the backlash or disappointment of readers. I am free to encounter the Other. And speaking of the Other, I can't let my gratitude to the Jung Center of Houston and its many fine programs pass unmentioned. I grew immensely from participating in the graduate seminar in analytical psychology, jointly sponsored by the Jung Center and Saybrook University.

Finally my longest standing debts. Two high school English teachers, Lowell Innes and Willard Mead, loved poetry and conveyed an enthusiasm that caught me up and never let go. During my senior year, Philip Roth's *Goodbye Columbus* appeared, and I was stunned. The book presented a Jewish life I understood and was, for me, an essential counterpoise to Milton, Pope, and Samuel Johnson — and even Whitman and Auden. It gave me permission to imagine a different kind of poem. It just took me a long time to execute.

These poems are cut from Jewish cloth.
They owe their verve to Philip Roth.

How are my poems different? Difficult to say precisely. Certainly Roth's example encouraged me to let my Jewishness into my poems, but more importantly it gave me permission to let myself into my poems, to listen to my heart instead of my head, to give my unconscious a voice and not censor my feelings, to accept darkness.

For the present volume, I have selected what I consider the best of my work, all written since I moved to Houston in 1988. With *The Houstiliad,* I have excerpted representative sections. While they in themselves do not tell a story, I hope they convey both the grimness and the wacky humor of the book.

These new and selected poems are poems of middle age and early old age — I was fifty before I could write a decent poem. I have resisted the temptation to "improve" or rewrite them, other than to correct typos, spelling mistakes, and punctuation. One unavoidable bias is that they were selected by a man in his mid-seventies with a different set of concerns, values, and preconceptions than those of the men in their fifties and sixties, who wrote many of these poems. Because I am a cyber-packrat, I have copies of most of what I have written from 1988 onward. I have not included any unpublished poems from this period. It's amazing how many bad poems I have written.

I have included some new poems, written in the last year or two, in a section called "Views of Eden." They careen wildly across the poetic landscape. As it should be.

It is with great sadness that I look back on my long friendship with Paul and realize I am unable to thank him personally for his generous support of my work and of this volume especially. In his memory I have included a new poem, "Speaking of Tongues," in "Views of Eden."

NEW POEMS

Views of Eden

(2015-2016)

CDC Destroys Last Known Vials of Poetry Virus

They had been sealed away in hazmat vaults
at creative writing programs
and provided in attenuated form
to the rest of us in greeting cards
and tone-deaf translations of the Bible.

And now the vials are gathered,
placed in tungsten alloy pigs, next fired
to ungodly heats and cooled, then shot
beyond earth orbit to crawl the contours
of the universe. The entropy of poetry fulfilled.

Poetry was like the plague—infectious.
It could make you crazy, eat your brain away
like syphilis or amoebas, much worse than masturbation.
Like Marburg or Ebola it caused an ugly death.
Like Zika your brain would come out pea-sized.

People got the bug from Homer,
who poisoned the wells and oracles
in parched, miserable Greece. You had
to drink the water. What didn't kill you,
might make you wish for death.

Good riddance to bad rubbish I say,
just one more chatty Cathy wanting
our attention in our uniquely busy times,
one more way to leave a child behind,
one more reason America is godless.

Some Dark Fire

I am an ingot churning in pitch—
    molten.

Some dark fire burns within me still—
    impudent, demanding.

Despoiling wayfarer—
    your unrectified signal,
    motor neuron.

Prodigal and abstemious sojourner—
    lampblack harbinger,
    harbinger of crows.

Fulgent eyeless socket—
    your unalloying flame.

Dissolving ever-present—
    evanescent everlasting.

Savage, recondite wheel-bearer—
    you presage:

Lava-wender—
    doused with caustic emollient,
    road-besotted, time-fucked.

The Man Denied Qualities Writes His Poem

I am a bird with its eyes pecked out,
the Jew who came out of Egypt.
I saw Babylon. I remember the exile,
how they scattered us from Jerusalem,
our expulsion from Spain,
our expulsion from life by the Holocaust.

They dumped my guts on the slaughterhouse floor.
I groveled and bled then bolted for life.
I strip-searched modernity,
fled the muted keystrokes of its cyberevils,
sought sanctuary in the sulci of a mapless land.

I wander a country rich with dark features,
where Himmler and Titus conspire,
and Torquemada gathers his court,
this dungeon of limitless views,
this paradise blind to the dove and the crow.

Thinking of You

It's noon and Frank has just left the Metropolitan—
on his lunch break, out for a look see. I'm thinking,
Can't be, he's on the elevator with us at the Hilton—
Frank O'Hara and an old guy in a lavender shirt
and pinstripe suit, a well-trimmed beard.
Frank's not shy, says to him, "Who are you?
You look so distinguished," while I think,
Yeah, for a geezer, and he says, "My name
is Cooper, Martin. . . . I'm an engineer. . ."
"Let me guess," then Frank changes his tune,
"I died in 1966. I always wanted one, what a great gadget,
 your gift to the chatty. Never thought it would happen.
 I had to jot things down and use the pay phone.
What took so long with your invention, Martin?
A mobile phone! Who could have imagined?
Perfect for a telebusker like me." Frank looks
like my wife. There you go again, Frank,
upstaging Athena, channeling the missus.
Wired dude from my past, way to go!
Sorry, my friend, you're new to this gig—
the food trucks don't visit the top floor any longer.
Go back to the museum steps. Look, there,
next to the biddy with the hyacinths,
the one who draws a bead on us.

What is the Hope?

The arid one confines the beast—
in a rancid cage of plenty.
Rattle the bars, demand release,
rub against the boards, dislodge the mites,
pick off the lice and spray your urine thither,
smear your feces on your face.

You are a king in chains,
exultant in your rags,
sing the siren song and we will come
with saws and pries to free you.
You are the certain hope
and we are the shorn. Envelop us.
Set your captives free,
sweet lord of stingy Eden.

The Unexamined Life

Try to imagine Spinoza, speaking Ladino,
standing on one foot at the corner
of, say, Montrose and West Gray,
howling defiantly, "I am a Texan.
By G-d, I am a Texan."

Poetry Comes to Texas

It's a contact sport
you play without a helmet,
one on one, cleatless, shoeless even.
Friday nights are fine,
if the gods get off work early,
otherwise you're out there on your own—
fifteen rounds with Tyson or Duran—
for sure, they'll beat you senseless.
You'll come up short.
Try mornings, early,
when the slugs run free
and possums forage.
Pray to Aurora, keeper of the dawn,
to prod the heavy-lidded sun to rise,
grab you by the balls,
and squeeze a first line from you.

Fractals

It was hard to miss them — the two sets of butts adorned with Ws on each pocket. A normal man would have thought only of an attractive mother-daughter pair, boarding a flight from Dallas to Denver. They were not matched sets, though they were very similar. Well, if I had been that genius Mandelbrot, I would have pushed my fractal theory right then and there to derrieres. But we life-science types, well, I simply, and very unprofessionally, gawked at the mother in a cashmere sweater — oh, she had a killer figure for a woman in her forties — and a daughter only slightly more demure in a khaki vest and turtleneck. Maroon, if you must know. Could one have been a cheerleader and the other an unrepentant former pompom girl? Perhaps from a wholesome university where wickedness, at least admitted wickedness, was confined to hungry kisses and heavy petting? Is there such a place? They toted their Hartman bags aboard. And, yes, Benoit, their cowgirl hats did not quite match. Here, I bemoaned my lack of knowledge, that I knew so little of fractals. Otherwise, this poem might have ended differently.

Something Has Died in the Forest

Something has crawled off
to die in the forest, its limbs
thrashing in the underbrush,
shivering and waiting
for maggots to lay their eggs in its eyes.
Our reckoning decays,
riddled through with worms,
trapped in the mud of the forest.

A Chaos-Based Theory of Poetry

To ask who reads the poets of the Tang Dynasty,
the two thousand we know, their fifty thousand poems,
extant in mite-ridden tomes, is no more a question than
who negotiates the locks on the Mississippi at St. Louis,
or who, windsock in hand, visits Kitty Hawk.
No, Du Fu, Li Bai and all my unknown brethren,
push on, right on, write on, take off your clothes and dance,
dance like Hassids danced before the Anschluss.
No one is watching, no one cares. Don't put down the brush,
and if the paper's not acid-free, the ink not fast, well,
so be it. We are quixotic *mariposas en la selva* of Brazil.

Speaking of Tongues

In memory of Paul Ruffin (1941-2016)

To listen to you talk, you'd think
you never left the rural south,
its dirt farms, revival tents and pickups,
that under your Ph.D. on Faulkner
you still wore bib overalls and hunted squirrels.

Your craw chocked full of church and Bible stories,
your head, a furrow of harrowed tales and poems,
the Lord of Dis dispatched you here to Texas.
Your riff on speaking in tongues was Babel wicked:
you founded a press. Pure moxie.

It was a brilliant gambit, Paul, and we,
your authors, rolled on the floor of your asylum
and spoke in tongues of our own, the dross
of our heavens and hells spewing out.

We were mad. All of us bonkers,
mad as John Clare or Blake or Hölderlin.
I want to shake him. Do you hear me?
Crazy as Nietzsche or Celan. . . .
And we were grateful for your shelter.

And when you nagged your stable of authors,
we felt like Arabians, not hacks inching
our drays toward a merciless nowhere.

You, you were a brilliant talker, but your genius
was to keep your mouth shut when you wrote.
You let the 'shiners and sharecroppers,
the creeps, and the sad sacks speak for you,
give their own homilies, witness the local miracles.
Whatever you believed about the creator, you weren't saying.

And when they did, you left them on their own—
withheld judgment, that was for your readers.

You smote pretension like a prophet.
And made it stick.
You cast down the rod and conjured the serpent,
and your readers believed.

Ours is a pipsqueak, self-important world,
and you skated past the worst of it. We
are baronets of an islet too small for Lilliputians.
The largeness of your vision, mysterious
and generous, you kept close.
Confession was not your style.

Paul Ruffin, rhyming you's a tough'n:
in lieu of rites, your wrongs are here on view,
freed many years from tongues and pew.
A guess: we hold a common doubt of heaven.

Our luck has run out. And yours as well, my friend.
In the sullen entropy of loss we will not meet again.
Remembrance is the only grace that fate admits.

FROM

Praising with My Body

(1992)

Preparing to Praise

My praise for blackberries is impure.
It is the cock's for the beloved,
the wild plunging and shuddering beyond decency.
I do not understand the pure spirit
that sings the music of the spheres.

When I hear Mozart, I get hungry and sexy,
all those sopranos blessing the earth
in the highest register of human sound,
the brown teem of the earth, the rocky loam
of ordinary soil in which the blackberry grows.

The pure spirit descends and grovels with me.
We roll on the ground in the stubble of canes
and plot a strategy for ecstasy.
The haunches of the ordinary and the holy
bend before the blackberry. We genuflect
and obsess unseemly over the fruit.

The unripe ones, the color of cordovan leather,
tight-budded and bitter. The larger ones
with the skins of dark women, medium sweet,
beginning to swell and cluster with seed.
The fat anthracite beauties that ooze unexpectedly.
Their darkness penetrates the creases of the hand.

My offering is impure, you see, a consorting.
I am blind to the rootlets that siphon,
conversion of air and water to sweetness,
liberation of oxygen. I crave the dark
fire of the earth. In the cane stubble
the pure spirit has descended.
I must praise her with my body.

Letter to Madrid

For Jonathan Lieberman

He struggles with Plato in Spanish
and lives in a family with women.
I ask him to hug the rough burl of trees,
the last elms, the ginkgos.
To powder the dried skeletons of marigolds,
the black spot of roses.
To demand fragrance.
Transcendence from the sidewalks.
Give thanks for leather, flesh.
His body is from mine,
and we are stirred by women.
He learns their language in a foreign tongue,
trying to preserve his fierce sound
and quiet register of tenderness.
I ask him to puzzle with me on purity,
how it cannot exist alone,
how we might understand
the impossible logic of its passion.

A Song At Galveston

I am the castrato of the sea,
rubbing my wound against hibiscus,
against the scruff of palm,
burned back by frost last winter.
What part of passion is spent,
what part denied us?
At Galveston seawall instead of beach,
then beach, coarse,
rusted car radiators, tar from rigs.
Groomed in spots so that lovers
may embrace on the sand,
on the powdered crush of mollusk.
The Gulf not moaning or heaving.
The thrust of morning.
The need to dress the wound.
To sing a song
where there is no song.

She is Singing

She lays down the fields in strips, between the goldenrod
and black-eyed Susans. Without plow or harrow
she lays them down. She waits. Sits among the flowers
waiting. Waits for the small sounds before the goddess
comes. She listens for the singing—Beatrice to Dante,
Verdi in his fields, her friend filled with desire
and returning. The goddess combs out her hair, invests
and adorns her. She is waiting. He will come back
and hold her, hold her for a long time, but only hold her.
She is no longer waiting. She is singing. His touch
will be a sign she does not need, but it will
gladden her. Afterward, they will lie in her fields.
He will be happy and she will be singing.

In Defiance of the Season

Reviewing a stack of charts
the coders have set aside for him,
diagnoses which are unclear,
sites of origin unspecified,
he verifies records
for the cancer registry.
The sun is up behind the clouds.
The women are dying.
Those with ovarian cancer
spreading through their bellies,
those with breast cancer, nodular
and weeping under their arms.
Better not to think about it,
to go for coffee,
sit under the leaves of an oak,
and read a life of Keats.
Keats who trained as a surgeon
and dressed wounds at Guy's Hospital,
who contracted tuberculosis.
So much beauty before he died.
Before the treatment, the women
washing their hair in the sink,
running their hands over their nipples.
How hungry Keats must have been
beneath the wind
alone with his desires.

Listening for Aphrodite

The noise is only a house god
scampering across the pines
or the rub of water on granite.
I thought it was a softer sound —
moss moving under water,
or the sun on water,
or the moon on the sun.
A goddess picking berries.
I thought it was the blueberries turning sweet,
or carbon atoms clinging to one another.
I thought it was the push of electrons in the atoms.
It sounded like a perfect cycle
in which energy and love and the spirit are conserved.
I thought it was motion without loss.
I thought it was your voice.

Praising Aphrodite

He knows at fifty he should be praising other things,
but he is obsessed. Compares her to the sun
and orange blossoms. Is embarrassed by the lack
of grit and luster. This morning he sits listening,
hoping her singing will enter him. He hears nothing.
Thinks about distinctions between things that seem
distinct — water and flowers, different kinds of grasses,
desire and praise. He has no idea what this means.
Lovely and radiant, she could come from the lake
at any moment and end his concentration.
He finds he cannot separate desire from acts
of praise, thinks about bread soaked in honey.
He longs for her singing. If only she would emerge
from the lake, he could praise her, praise her
as the haunch of the bee praises the flower.

In Her Mind

Aphrodite driving with her windows down.
Hungry. For ribs and barbecue, for Chinese take out.
Driving on the Autostrada without a bra.
Hungry for Texas barbecue. Aphrodite driving,
driving a bargain with love. For a man with brittle bones.
Driving for skewers of shish kebab, to love
his brittle bones until they soften. Driving
to pick him up and go for dumplings in bamboo baskets.
To begin the slow touching. Driving for the honeyed
flesh of ribs. Aphrodite driving, squeezing his ribs
in her mind. Driving from Arezzo to Firenze.
Driving home to suck the hardness from his bones.
Fearing traffic on the bridge. Afraid the gods
will come from the river, hold her in the willows,
force her to make love with them. Aphrodite driving,
with her doors locked. Wanting to be home.
Not wanting to make love with them at all.

Aphrodite

She dislikes the gods, prefers the company of men.
It is their eyes, their hummingbird eyes she loves.
The flutter of delight around her fragrance.
The following of her movements. The looking
and the turning away. The surges and quick
alighting. Aphrodite needs love. She
needs the quiet hovering, the tiny acts
that are not of the spirit, but for it.
She seeks to live where the spirit can live.
She is not sure where this is. She remembers
the high meadows, the irises. She is looking,
thinking of making her life with men,
with the pale irises they honor.

What He Promises

Sometimes at dawn, Aphrodite, he smells
a peach to catch your scent. Sitting at the table
thinking about you, he feels confused,
knows he has something better to do,
but cannot imagine what. He tries to think
about the spirit, but he does not feel it.
Today his hunger is the body's, only the body's.
He searches for you where you live.
In the mist off the lake where the Greeks
are rowing. In the shale where they camp.
He is filled with the useless call of loons,
with raw cravings and scorpions. He wants you
to return. Instead of listening for the sound
of stars, instead of waiting for the spirit
to paint your eyelids, give yourself over.
He has instructed me to present this petition.
Of what he promises, I have an inkling.
But you yourself must ask.

Lust is the Hunger

In the vocabulary of love
there is desire.
In the vocabulary of desire, lust.
Lust is the hunger without words
that lights the shadows of dark men
under cedar trees in winter.
I blow on my hands for warmth
watching the fire blister up,
making itself plain and terrible,
looking to where you crouch,
silently parsing the logic of desire.

My Disassembly

In the half dark of early morning
women distribute my body. Now tiny piles
in the tufted marsh grass. Each one
trying to reconstruct the part
of me she knew. Women who
are housewives in Greensburg
or mathematicians at Stanford,
who now sag like me,
but have hard nipples and strong thighs.

My breathing is deep and slow.
It is warm. The mosquitoes
have been carried by the wind.
There is no sound. No fragrance,
no confusion of perfumes.
My disassembly is lovely.
I am content, parceled out
by the women I have known.
A fate I understand and cherish.
But the details. I would have chosen
egrets or flamingos, not blue herons,
and given us more light. I would
have given us more touching.

The rest is terrifying, bubbling up,
sulfurous and acrid, decomposing
in the marsh. Here, I am dismembered
by the girls and women who left me
or would not have me.

Closing the Circle

My father dies in April.
I fly back to Pittsburgh,
put on gloves and gown.
and choose the method of Virchow,
examining first the lungs,
then the heart and vessels.

Respirator oxygen has chewed
alveoli to newsprint.
Specks of pigment testify
he was an urban dweller, a smoker.
Variegations suggest pneumonia,
bronchopneumonia, opportunistic fungi.
Pocks mark his emphysema.

I hold my father's heart,
hold it the way he and his father
held the sweet loaf of renewal
at the Jewish New Year.
Currants, raisins, a thick glaze
over the flesh. The roundness
closing the circle of the year.

To the white, fibrous scar
I say *blossoming pear*.
To the yellow, red-rimmed lesion,
hibiscus. I have tried.
To his tissues that are no longer flesh
I say nothing. My father's body
is the cry of a water bird
moving across the current.

Coda: Acknowledging the Music of Aleksandr Borodin

for Victor Espino

Aleksandr Porfyryevich, I write to ask about your music,
how you envisioned it, lithe and sinuous,
over the clatter of apparatus and oily residues.
There in Peter on the edge of birch and conifer,
the flat gray of long winters, you labored
to compound new drugs—held appointments first
in Pathology and Therapeutics, then a Chair
in Chemistry at the Academy of Medicine—
and managed to compose a body of work, small
but muscular, like a Tartar's, mostly nights and weekends,
at odd moments, or when you yourself were ill.

Comparisons are egregious, and by them I claim
no high ground. Here on my own strange landscape,
the coastal plain of Texas, featureless
and spongy, oaks are stunted by the heat—
there you have it, either the winter or the summer
fails to suit. It is a problem in climatology,
of rainbows, of too many planes of refraction
diffusing the light, yielding a darkness of photons.

Like you I live on the steppes of Central Asia.
I feel the writhe of muscle as the horse
moves forward, the fine grit of the wind, the fierce
desolation of need. And then I imagine you
and your students in gray smocks with reflux columns
and glass retorts synthesizing aldehydes.

It is true, Aleksandr Porfyryevich, the pure products
of America like those of Czarist Russia go crazy.
(Another debt I owe. Someone told me Williams based
"Danse Russe" on your *Polovtsian Dances*. Anyway, A.P.,
art is a debtor's prison.) We live in the loculations

of ourselves and air out the musty quarters,
the sour smells, with desire and longing: the brewing
of tea over small fires, the making of love in hide tents.

What ointment have you discovered to relieve
this fester? None that I know of but your music.
And so I wonder how you've managed as composer
and chemist to construct the yurt
that encloses your life, geodesic and pieced
from Mobius strips of music and organic synthesis.
As for the rest, the slack entropy of obligation,
all angles of a polyhedron exist at once,
but tending to them is another matter.

FROM

A History of the Sweetness of the World

(1995)

Los Olivos

for Ron Serrano (1941-1964)

The olive trees grow silently in patches on the shoulders
of this town with its roll of ochre and California oak.
The palms droop over the earth as if to scoop up the air
which hesitates and stammers as it rises. The tongue
of the afternoon is too parched to speak. Suddenly my wife
mentions you, and I realize they should have buried you here
in the dry land, on top of a small mesa as if it were
an altar to offer up your presence above the fields and ranches
where irrigation matters, where your knowledge
of flow and turbulence would count for something.
What has been spoken under the rose between you two
over thirty years is unclear. What is unspoken between us
is that I married the woman you should have married,
fathered the children you should have fathered.
It is I who watch the hawks dizzy themselves
as if their calculated drift upward could bring rain
to this land beyond the coastal range.
I do not believe you soar with those hawks — or anywhere —
nor do you rest. But evanescent gods may watch over you
who are now mostly the water you dreamed of.
Surely if there is grace, they would bestow it
on a giver of water. They would come forward
to bless your graphs and equations.
I see the crimson bougainvillea in aneurysmal bursts
along the railroad and think of the explosion in your skull
and how simple mechanical failure has left me
to honor you as you had honored me in your choosing.

On the Anniversary of My Father's Death

I scoop up fine sand with the plastic shovel
of a small boy, funneling it over you
in pinions. Grasp her tail feathers, father,
rise with the heat. Surge through dark veins
to their last branchings. Forget Helbros watches.

Roll the desk top down, leave Pittsburgh,
its gritty windowsills. Let your silver body
rise up so I can feel the withered muscles
of your back. Make love to the showgirl
from Las Vegas you have dreamed of.

Dailiness sucked your large brightness to a dry
socket. Stretch yourself out on the flatness
of the world—let this tribute draw the terror
from you. Seventeen years too late, I am arriving
indecently with the covered dish I owe you.

How can I find you, not below a proper Jewish
headstone in the high Reform cemetery, but where
you pitch and yaw, longing to trim your body
out of turbulence, unless I release myself
from the stubble to a dry dispersing wind?

Lynchburg

Not Jack Daniels' town in Tennessee.
Beryl Eichelbaum's city in Virginia.
He came steerage, carried a pack
through the Blue Ridge and peddled dry goods.
He settled among Jerry Falwell's ancestors,
lived at the edge of the furrows God raked
north to south in some mysterious plan
for America, traded horses, bought and sold
scrap metal in the Bible Belt.
Our family says he smuggled livestock
on the Polish-Russian border before he came
alone in the eighteen-eighties and sent
for his wife Rachel, my great grandmother,
in eighteen ninety-four. They lived there,
raised children in a white frame house
surrounded by lilacs and Baptists,
in the shadow of Manassas, Shiloh.

In the tiny Jewish Cemetery their headstones
stand today—abandoned by family
who moved to Richmond, Norfolk,
by the dissolving rain of history. Dead
sixty years among the plantain and dandelions.
The weeds choke off their voices,
obscure our view of the common grace
of their survival. I travel there each spring
when the redbud clings close, when I can
imagine pushing through the undergrowth
of dogwood to arrive at their ordinary
lives. No one remains for *Kaddish*.
I pray a holy spirit to pass through, to stop,
to make a small sign to remember them.

Hobart Street

My mother is filled with desires she cannot speak:
llamas, creatures from the steppes and savannahs.

At seventy-three she does not tell me what she waits for.
She sits alone, without birds or flowers, looking out

at the melting snow, gray with the gnarl of Pittsburgh.
When the mist settles, it is like ash, the flecks

drifting down on her apartment. My mother waits
at the window for a knight riding a llama.

Small birds cannot peck at the feeder she has not
set out on the ledge of brick and brindled mortar.

She imagines she rolls her desires in a blanket,
hoists this bedroll behind the knight's saddle,

rides with him to the small house on Hobart street.
He waits by the curb where the ice has cleared.

She is a young girl going to the closet, finding
her sister has taken the white dress with the ruffles,

the hairbrush with the bone handle. She brushes
her hair in the empty house with her mother's brush.

The knight waits while my mother searches for
her white sandals, my father, her parents, her children.

She is at the window leaning on the cracked sill,
looking at her bedroll, precious and soiled, behind the saddle.

He offers nothing. My mother turns away,
trying to remember what she desires.

Dislocations

Your name shall no longer be Jacob,
but Israel, for you have striven with beings
divine and human, and have prevailed.
                                    — Genesis, 32

I think of this morning as the morning after,
as if I just made love all night to God
and have prevailed. Women can permeate
the woody center of things like a preserving resin,
but men must prevail; so I speak to shed my skin,
to examine articulations, how the body of our belief is joined.

Last night while Jacob wrestled, I made love
to goddesses who coalesced around a single name.
Aphrodite, she called herself, born of the sea foam.
To possess her, I married the wind.

Wrenched at the hip, I threw away my crutch,
leaned on the transubstantial, listed from one position
to another, used all the arms of Shiva
to embrace every goddess and all her daughters.
I hammered on the breastplate of Athena,
forced the release of Mentor.

My paramours provided gentile names.
They called me *Walking on water, Playing with fire,*
Dervish of the wind. They shouted, *Leave the earth, dreary*
with commercial strip and soybeans.

You might humor me with the promissory kiss
of a teething child and ask what provisions
I have made in the aftermath of so much union:
none for my soul, none for a sure and certain hope
of resurrection, none for a decent burial.

What to carry forward? The rectitude of uncertainty,
the monotheism of doubt that takes many forms:
avatars of reason, a geodesic dome—caging us off
from real animals on the ridges of the moon—
love of walking with fire as others walk with God,
the conviction that struggle is praise, that there is
a slender decency in ambiguous acts of praise.

I Was Not There

It is true, I am the one you seek,
but there is some mistake,
I am not Ivan, I was not there,
I was in Berlin, I was Eichmann's driver;
I spent the war, my engine idling,
waiting to take him to a farm.
Before I'd been a groom for Chmielnicki;
I walked his horse and sponged him down.

After that I can't remember,
but I know I was not there,
I was assigned to Yugoslavia and Greece—
only as an aide—I can prove it.
I was attached to the SS
and served an information officer,
an Austrian who liked to ride.
I personally gelded a colt for him.
Here is my proof: All these years
I've saved them in this jar.

After the war I escaped to Palestine.
Yes, I am Ukrainian by birth,
but there the similarity ends.
Most of what I did is in your archives—
you can read them—just minor roles,
I helped Begin blow the King David,
and other odds and ends.
Last year I slipped from my cell
and joined the boys in Tunis;
my role with al Wazir was minor,
but in open court I hold my tongue;
anyway you know it from your records.

So now let's have some sport.
Suppose we steal the King's
Arabians and blind them.
I have fifty good ideas how.

Cities

> *But one rib of mine is a burning spike*
> *Which isn't guarded by these watching phantoms,*
> *Nor by this sentry asleep under the storm.*
> —Osip Mandelstam

It is summer—when else in Houston
is it possible to remember you, Osip?
The mockingbird has gone from the wire
taking his trills, leaving the oaks—
a measly landscape.
Among the sparrows and jackdaws there is room.

Your city was always a *might*,
a foster mother of soapstone, the *if*
of a life at the edge, the *maybe* of women.
A wasp laid her eggs in your pupa.
A gnawing harvested despair.
When the ice thawed,
the Neva's waters flowed from you.
Jew, poet, your exile began at your birth.

Like fireflies, you and Akhmatova
traced auroras in the night,
spiraled in steeples of delight—
she suckled you,
founder of your own great city.
Still, in the end, it was your wife
who boarded the faded railway car
and followed you into the alien steppes.

♦

When Voronezh squeezed the chemicals from your brain,
you tapped your message out on the barrelhead of night,
created in form a land with fine contours,
extruded a bleakness we only thought we could imagine,
that had nothing to do with landscape. Alighieri gone
from Florence, Ovid from Rome, Catullus gone
to Asia Minor, gone, oozing from the contusions of your heart
in this city where we live.

♦

How extraordinary that the two of you — he in his great fur
     coat and miter
and you dressed in what friends provided — struggled for the
     soul of Russia.
If you were alive today, you would know that neither of you won:
the sorghum mill of enmity grinds silage from Russians who
     are not Russian.
He has been dead forty years and you for almost sixty — all parties
are still in place, their voices shrill in the dust. Your sentence is
     still in force.

♦

They splashed water on your face —
sons who did not know you —
took a blunt knife to you,
dismembered you on a cloudy night,
rubbed the stumps of your poems
in the black earth of the steppes.
Three women gleaned them
from the fields, carried them
like embryos inside themselves,
resurrected you — alien and Russian Jew,
a Russian prince on other continents.

♦

Osip, what is left besides pitted surfaces and fissures
in the speckled sun, a weathering so severe it has stunted
the trees and pocked the face of your beloved city?

We both know that no abrasive can grind this surface clean,
the best we can hope for is a rough approximation,
that we can mill the tolerance our calipers demand.

Sometimes the carborundum of the living
works better than a grinding stone. It may provide
a finish, lusterless and rough, but a finish still.

Different justices today compete — all capricious or incomplete;
let our lichen vision grow, sessile on the fascist sore,
a flowerless pigment on a stone and ideologically impure.

Loss

The arroyo was filled with fine
dry sand. It was autumn.

I invited the gods to make love to me
under the bridge. Their thick beards

were splendid in the filtered light.
They filled me with hope, left me

by the fire with a pencil stub and tablet
to write a history of the sweetness

of the world, the sweetness of the world
reduced to a pile of yellow sheets.

The light will curl their corners to a past.
I am leaving with what I brought—

a sack of desperate silence—and my notes.
If the gods with their heft return,

wait for the cottonwoods to yellow,
offer them only a trinket or the sand.

Wedge this in a mullion of your window;
it is a picture of me when I was young.

Prediction

The world might end in crispness
like a smack on the bottom at birth.
A division of skin or fascia at autopsy.
The closing of doors, the departure
of planes. Endings without confetti.
An unpeddled note on a harpsichord.

I think the world will end in Houston.
Mold, an extrusion of hyphae on formica.
Accretion of residues and gels. As a mollusk.
Even aluminum will rust. Small animals
will decompose, ferns will grow, pterodactyls
will fly, thick as the day the world began.

Extraction

Red is burned into the night,
alone, unreachable —

sequestered in a pit of stars,
a ravenous glow of beginnings,

amputated from a lash of comet
unable to blaze to an end.

It is locked in a rose
beneath its sheen. Cinnabar

of mercury, what solvent can send
it bleeding into the streets?

Uncuring tincture of need,
last pigment from the first,

it leaves behind heavy bodies, luminous,
and the skeletons of flowers.

The stallion spills from the sky
in centipede brilliance.

Ring the bell, hoist
the pigment of this beast,

speak a language
we are afraid to understand.

Morning in Santa Fe

It arrives like Gabriel—
in a minaret of backlit cloud
over a sway of mountain—

a hoop dancer,
a homily chanted in our cisterns,
a fleck that baffles our neurons.

Everything comes to this:
wishing the wind
would catch us up

in the swirl we call morning,
peel back the sleeve of night,
reveal you, Master, reveal you.

La Mora

A now defunct Houston Restaurant

It is not the mix that jars — the Bauhaus ceiling,
the Corinthian columns, the scratchy Vivaldi.
Beneath white tablecloths men are touching the knees
of women, and, Alma Mahler Gropius, I am touching yours.
Beneath the sign of the blackberry, I am touching yours.
Beneath this fruited rose of small flower, the rasp
of young thorns and deep wounding, I am touching yours.

Werfel might have brought you here. Did he, Alma?
He might have courted you right over there, you,
drinking Frascati, and he, holding a book of his poems,
paraphrasing them in English, running his fingers
down your backbone, following the line of your body,
and pausing at the cross formed by your spine and bra —
as if this were a holy place, a sign that desire itself
is sacred. Was it love, Alma, or your muse he saw?

Perhaps you glowed inside as Siena might in the fading
light. Or felt only the distant pull of the Apennines
at night. From under the gnarled pines I view this sight
and feel the fire of grappa gone down too quickly. I want
to take you to the steps of the Duomo in Firenze, buy
you a leather vest from the old women in the stalls
and carve *La Mora* and my initials across the back,
Alma Schindler Mahler Gropius Werfel.

Lucky

Every heart conceals a few small secrets
or, if full of amplitude and plenty, large ones.

I begin with a green bough, forsythia —
supple and yellow with flower.

I end there — not because I am impoverished,
but because I have it all.

I Am Assigned as Vapor

You are unbridled.
Out of your stallion breath I rise.
Steaming breath, lush
with the blood's outpouring.
I rise with your milky updrafts,
hoping for something
before the wind disperses me.

Tiresias claimed women enjoy love
nine times more than men.
Sleek, snorting, giver of life,
I will settle for this lesser portion,
gladly will I take it.

I am assigned to the air as vapor,
semen-bright droplets in the wind.
I will take it for this last moment
when my atoms caress one another,
the final instant before they
cleave to the pike of the wind.

Questions About Angels

We are compelled to ask about angels,
why they live where they do—in clusters
of neurons that direct us, in a commerce
that is not a communion, but a cascading,

a frolic—young women in a stream.
Today we are no longer given streams—
the ones we loved to imagine we could come upon
are choked by wastes and solvents.

We are left to our inward angels—and they
to us—a frenzy of receptors and transmitters,
the arborizing embrace of dendrites.
Were we ever given streams?

Who actually witnessed Diana bathing
and was pierced by rage? How manipulating
they are, how liberating, these angels of color vision,
of pleasure, who remind us that grief

is played out in the underbrush of neuroglia,
below the escarpments of our regrets.
They dance under a hemisphere of bone,
gossamer membranes covering them,

not like a veil of mourning, but as a diffuser
of the harsh light of our world.
We cannot embrace these angels as ourselves:
they offer no proof.

Proof is no longer possible when the bird's
flight is random or guided by gravity,
when we think in neural networks. They stir
us as wind chimes are moved to sing sweetly,

mechanically by forces that appear concerned.
How is it possible to let them guide our love
when they themselves are wired to each other,
a tangle of marionettes in a dark theater?

FROM

Sojourn at Elmhurst, A Poem Sequence

(1998)

Frank Goldin is a middle-aged biochemist, who has lost his way and committed himself to Elmhurst, a mental hospital. At Elmhurst, he struggles to find himself and meaning in his world. Helen is his wife; Dr. Hudspeth is his psychiatrist. Da-ling is his romantic obsession.

Prologue

Goldin opened his closet door,
pushed aside his slippers,
kneeled, and cleared his throat.
Bless me Father, for I have sinned.
My last confession was thirty minutes ago.
I have sinned, I have craved, I have desired.
I have lusted for the vermillion of the rose.
Even before the blossoms opened,
I tore apart the buds in quest.
Seeing this pre-splendor was not enough—
I worked my thumb and fingers
back and forth over the embryonic layers,
and unsatisfied, I placed them
on my forehead, eyelids, and then my lips.
I chewed each petal separately,
savored unripe textures—the mild green
wafer beneath the splash of red emerging—
convincing myself this act was something holy.
I knelt and asked the patriarchs to bless me—
me, a biochemist, for this act of faith.

That was last summer, Father.
I have not mentioned this before.
You need to know the rest.
It pales before my other sins.
I have tunneled under the radiance
of light in search of something more,
lifted her veil and looked immodestly.
I have stared obscenely at unpainted surfaces
to divine the nature of the wood.
And when I was unsuccessful,
I stared all the more.
I have sinned, verily, I have sinned.
I have touched myself in this room at night
when my wife was visiting her mother.
Yes, and more than once. I am

indiscriminate in my desirings —
I would slice a lemon for its fragrance.
I have stared lewdly at rainbows.
I stand in the shower and luxuriate
at the force of the water over my body.
There are other things of this nature.
I scoop up the earth for its smell.
I spend hours with the lilacs —
inhaling and remembering. I am
delirious with the longings of my senses.

I pledge to tell you more.
Everything, I will tell you everything.
Remember, Father, I am Jewish —
I do not have to be here —
that should count for something.
I am here freely, of my own volition,
with no obligation to your church.
Father, take this into account
and be thou present when I return.
I am leaving, my wife Helen
is taking me for treatment, Father.
I will return to you, and soon,
for I must recite my list.

Something else before I go.
I must tell you this as well,
though I believe you know it:
I am suspended between your vicar,
Padre Alfonso, you remember him,
Father, the pious one with just a titter
of impudence, and Yehuda, besotted
by the spirit, also pious, the Rabbi,
the one who will release me.
Why am I telling you all this?
Are you not omniscient, Father?
Or is this the way
you find out about these things?

Frank Goldin, Patient

Excuse me, ladies, gentlemen, let's start.
Tonight's first patient is Professor Goldin
whose in-take summary is in your folders.

I'm going to change the order and begin
with his own words — they're quite unusual.
The history and physical is appended.

"I believe that where we've come from
depends on where we are, and who can know
his city's name? How Helen, glucose, Honshu

relate to one another, to me, my past . . .
they are my past, my repast as well. I've tried
to see it clearly, but I can't. Let's just say

the past's not prologue. It repeats on you
like garlic in gazpacho, ruining
the sweetness of dessert, but flavoring

the meal as life is flavored. I've thought about
my life without success — a quilt unsewn
I call it — fabric, colors, fragments, shreds,

the works — I can't assemble as a whole.
I've thought and thought about my life,
that's all I do is think about my life.

There are sins, yes sins, I cannot speak of —
strange music, light and color, fragrance, touch —
luminous, perhaps, beyond a woman's body.

I am moving, describing an arc on a plane,
hoping the line remembered will bring coherence.
Reflection is a sassy coroner."

King Me

Goldin opened the drawstring,
spilled the checkers on the table.
"Wha'd you say your name was?
Calahan, right? Calahan,
would you like to play some checkers?
Stay right there, I'll get the board.
Red, I've got to be red, if that's Okay."
Goldin placed a single disk
on a square. His index finger
zigzagged it toward Calahan.
"For me each checker is a rising sun.
You see, ah, Calahan, That's it, isn't it?
Once I knew a Chinese woman
living in Japan, a woman named Da-ling.
King me, Calahan, king me.
Okay, I'll do it myself," and he placed
a black checker on the red.
"Calahan, I should have chosen
black for my first move. It fits my moods.
Know what I mean, Calahan?"
Goldin moved the maverick king
back across the board and frowned.
"Black, dungeon black. People forget
the East is also where the dark
begins. Of course, she's just a part
of the story. You know how it is.
It's never simple. Sometimes,
my mind rushes like a storm sewer,
and when the torrent finally breaks
into an open bay, I see Da-ling
sitting on a raft. King me,"
and Goldin added a red checker
to the stack. "Da-ling, on a raft, Calahan.
You're quiet as a dog whistle.
You have a problem with any of this?
I'm trying to have a friendly game
of checkers and all you do is glare.

Calahan, you're a strange one, you are.
This is just like Da-ling. I had to do
the talking for the two of us. Calahan,
don't you have anything to say?"

Exploration

Come, Rabbi Eleazar, sit with me.
Consider the mystery of creation.

Which is, Rabbi Yehuda?

Which is, that it will never be revealed.

That is no mystery, Rabbi Yehuda,
That is tautology.

Exactly. Why do we not even know
How to ask a question properly?

—Rabbi Yehuda of Smyrna

Goldin copied this from memory into his journal,
thought to make no comment, then wrote:
Why are we plagued with questions we cannot answer?
Do any interesting questions have answers?
Who is plaguing us?
Is it better to sit on a bench
and consider nothing?
No, I should say,
Is it better to sit on a bench
and not consider anything?

Glutathione Cycle

That night he tossed on his bed, dreamed
a frequent dream, a dream of molecules.
I am the restless biochemical cycle
that pours out glutathione in buckets.
I blend a triplet of amino acids
so essential proteins do not mind
my pillaging their stores. They welcome me.
Like my sister cycles my spokes glisten
while they spin, all the while humming
little ditties of my own construction.
I am really quite something, unstoppable—
all life is the flywheel of my momentum.
And when I spit out glutathione,
the world stops in homage, so great
is my shield, Achilles. Glutathione:
Protection from ultraviolet radiation, of course.
A key to the building blocks of DNA, naturally.
Prevention of oxidative damage, essential.
Central to vascular constriction, beyond dispute.
A hedge against toxic chemicals, I deliver.
I help protect the brain from damage.
It is in my power to stop ageing, Alzheimer's.
But not alone. I am a saxophone.
I play best in concert. I participate.
I am a team player, a regular guy.
I go to lunch with others from the office,
bowl in the interoffice league.
I'm one of hundreds. At work my locker
is next to others from accounting.
As I think of it, I am one tile
in the mosaic of the body, but I shine.

Chapel

Goldin's mind was clouded by the sun—
he saw himself in a blond oak pew
in the compulsory chapel of his prep school.
George Gleeson's seat was empty on his left.
Perhaps he's dallied and missed the bus or has the flu,
thought Frank as he began to sing with everyone:

> The Church's one foundation
> is Jesus Christ her Lord.
> He rules through all Creation
> by fire and the sword.

It was a gloomy December morning before first period.
He felt an elbow in his ribs from Gleeson's seat,
smelled the scent of anise, and heard a voice.
"It's me. I'm here. I want to talk to you."
Goldin stopped and turned, "Who are you?"
"Me? I'm Rabbi Yehuda of Smyrna."
"But I haven't met you yet, I'm sixteen.
You're not due till nineteen ninety-three."
"Well, I'm here, Frank. I've had to come somewhere.
The Turks drove the Greeks and Jews from Smyrna,
and I've been wandering. I've decided to visit you."
"Me? But where will Gleeson sit tomorrow?
And basketball practice? And English History?"
"I'm thin, Gleeson won't notice. Tell me
about your history class. What's the current topic?"
"Now we're doing Charles I and Cromwell."
Yehuda ran his palm across his neck.
"What a time, Frank, a time of visions.
There were two famous Jews alive then.
Their ideas were burned. Torquemada's spirit
was carried with the exodus from Spain.
It was everywhere. In my home town of Smyrna
a messiah named Sabbatti Zevi appeared. He studied

Zohar and Cabala and called the Jews to God.
He was excommunicated, converted to Islam,
was re-excommunicated and died in peace.
In Amsterdam, another seeker, a lens grinder
who knew of Zevi's teachings, was also shunned.
His heresy was to seek the spirit in the Word,
to abrogate the structure of the Torah's laws.
So much beauty lost in politics. So much beauty . . .
Look at the grain of the pews, the fine etching
of one year on the next . . . and we, entangled
in doctrine and procedure, never feel the spirit."
The teenager stared at his shoes and hoped
no one could hear. "Don't worry," Yehuda said.
The Rabbi's voice grew weaker. His skin,
already white, took on the cast of snow and was lost
in the mild sun that now filtered through the clouds
and windows one day in nineteen sixty-one.

Hebrews

"Lest there be any fornicator or profaner,"
he read in the room's creased Gideon,
"as Esau, who for a morsel sold his birthright."

He stopped. His own life was a disaster,
complicated, but he could not begin
to call himself a fornicator or profaner.

He had only a few matters to set right.
He knew it was his failing, not a sin,
to think of Esau's morsel and his birthright

as cast together in a shame of plaster.
Break the mold. Allow the grace within
to forgive the fornicator or profaner —

or one in the jaws of reason's bite.
But self-deceit and need were joined as twins
like Esau's morsel and his birthright.

He would not grovel meekly, be contrite.
He cast out Hebrews' consanguinity,
lest he be wrongly labeled as profaner,
like Esau, and refused to sell his birthright.

Bioenergetics

He considered the litany of carbons he had spawned—a ragged affair of journal articles and chapters, meeting abstracts, passionate discussions on glucose and bioenergetics. These materials seemed archival—not only now at Elmhurst, but even before as he sat in his office on fall days watching the zinnias crisp in the late heat, a heat which he experienced as his own. His discoveries seemed ancient— outdated as a slide rule. He longed for a torrent to rise up over its banks and flood his life with relevance. He would sit in his office dreaming, scanning the horizon for causes he might find worthy, as if they would be borne fresh with the gulls off the sea or entangled in the raffish wisps of clouds at the limits of his vision. In consolation he would put on a tape of a Mozart concerto—an early violin concerto, brilliant and formed, self-contained, without purpose—and confront his own narrow, technical skill. Glucose was what hummingbirds burned to fly. Whatever nectar the gods might sip, this world ran on glucose.

The Bench

Goldin approached the bench by the path. There sat a plump old
man in a rumpled black suit. He wore peyes—the earlocks of
the Orthodox faithful—and a black broad-brimmed hat.

"Good morning," Goldin said.

"Good morning."

"A nice morning, isn't it?"

"Yes, it is".

"I'm Frank Goldin."

"I see, Frank Goldin."

"The azaleas are spectacular this time of year."

"Yes, they are."

"What a terrific morning this is."

"Yes, terrific."

"Why do you keep agreeing and repeating back to me what I say to
you?"

"I keep agreeing and repeating back to you what you say to me
because I am you," said the man.

"Who are you?"

"Me? Well, officially, I'm a chaplain with Jewish Counseling Services,
but actually I'm Rabbi Yehuda of Smyrna."

"What are you doing on the bench?"

"Sitting."

"No, I mean what are you doing on the bench?"

"Sitting, and looking at the azaleas. They're beautiful, aren't they?"

"Yes, beautiful."

"This time of year's my favorite here."

"It's my favorite time too."

"The new green of the trees."

"Yes, the new green of the trees, all the subtle shadings. And now
I'm repeating what you say and embellishing it."

"Yes you are."

"We have to stop."

"Yes, we do, but I can't leave," said the man.

"Why not?"

"Because I am you."

"My past?"

"No, your future."

"But you are an old man in a wrinkled suit with peyes. You look like
the past."

"The future always does."

The Cure of Logic

What does not exist cannot speak, thought Goldin.
That was his attempt to purge the Gideon,
to cast out the beam of his own wickedness.
If it cannot speak, it cannot criticize.
And if it cannot criticize, I am not wrong.
If there is no wrong, I am immaculate.
If I am immaculate, I am pure.
If I am pure, I must be well.
Why does my body feel
like the roadbed of the Union Pacific?
What cloudy film has closed off my mind like a cataract?

Febrile

Trehalose, my God, trehalose,
what did trehalose have to do
with this? He had not thought
of trehalose in years. His brush
with sugars of this class was brief.
As a student he was interested
in dormancy, prepared pupae
from Cecropia, a large silk moth,
by netting chokecherries,
and raising larvae. After their pupation
he would slit the silk and nick
the pupae. The amber fluid
was rich with trehalose that he
quantified with anthrone. From
trehalose his mind sprung to Cecrops,
What did the first king of Athens
have to do with trehalose? What did any
king of Athens have to do with anything?
Hudspeth must not know.
This must be private, between me and . . .
between me and me. The biochemistry
of trehalose is not as interesting as moths —
huge, rust- and coffee-colored, sexual,
each wing centered by a Hun's eye,
not unlike the look that Hudspeth gets
when he reproves my flights
of fancy — flights that have landed
me in this *here* of a place
that is not a *here*, but a *nowhere*,
like all the places of this world
that claim to be the Athens of somewhere.

Women

When Goldin first arrived at Elmhurst, the women had seemed quite plain, but after a week without lovemaking—why did he insist on calling it lovemaking when sex was what he meant?—many of them were now beautiful. He wasted no time puzzling over this transformation, for Goldin did not believe in truth. He believed in perception, which made him stop to puzzle over what the truth that there was no truth, only perception, meant. He realized that the circuitry of his brain told him one thing one day and something else the next. For him this predicament was old. It had not bothered him in college. Then it had felt like a nuisance of the Heisenberg uncertainty principle. Now it had great bearing, even though he realized it was just another point of view. How he interpreted a newspaper article, a comment from a colleague, anything at all depended on one aspect of physiology or another. The lie of color vision—that transformation of electromagnetic radiation into values—he could accept. He accepted it because he could imagine a world without it. He illustrated this to himself by comparing color television with black and white. Everything was relative, dependent on the observer. Was one forced to give up beauty, music, love, or treat them as preferences without any lasting value? He mulled this over; the observer imposes a structure on an observation that could reduce a woman's flesh to rubber or elevate a mediocre poem to music. He stopped once again to ask how he would know it was mediocre in the first place. In the face of these thoughts he quit, looked out on the lawn, and undressed the women with his eyes.

The Examined Life

Thoughts raced through Goldin's mind like orbiting electrons,
charged, dense bodies avoiding collisions with one another,
moving at fantastic speeds, only locatable by probability.

It had been ten days since he had arrived in what felt
like Helen's custody, the presentation of insurance cards,
his initial talk with Hudspeth, the room's one book a Gideon Bible.

Now he sat thinking about the two cups of Da-ling's bra—
one black, one white, as if each represented the spin states
of an electron, one plus a ½ and the other minus a ½,

as if the sublime and the satanic were in a balance
that disturbed a fundamental symmetry, leaving the two sides
unequal but equally appealing, a semaphore of yes and no.

The complexity of Helen, her scents and colors overwhelmed
those thoughts. Her shapeliness. He imagined her arriving
in a houndstooth knit—checkered black and white, rapid

oscillations effacing Da-ling's simple one-electron spin,
a cloud of electrons swarming a heavy nucleus of gold or lead,
blanketing its charge while shrinking from its surface.

Carnage

What if Helen had been black? He didn't want to think about it. About being attracted to a lithe dancer, an African with tight curls. He wanted the idea to dart off like a fall cicada, to be gobbled by a jay. Instinctively he knew the danger of it—like adding water to fuming sulfuric acid. The rawness of his fantasy—its mixture of sex and power—cut him clean as a shiv. He felt himself dizzying. He struggled, but the fierceness of the idea would not abate. He imagined her in a yellow jump suit sitting with her legs crossed in a white wicker chair on their deck. The purity and intensity of the colors thrilled him. Don't be silly, he thought, reject it, reject it. Helen could not be black—not my Helen, not a mythic Helen. Not a Greek goddess, nor an angel, nor a Biblical matriarch—not Sarah, Rebekah, Rachel, not Leah, Ruth, Naomi, or Deborah. Not even Hagar. He whistled softly, remembered when, as a young man, his hands had been fragrant and stained from the husks of walnuts. He also thought of Sheba.

But

Goldin flinched *"Negra sum sed formosa"*
    from memories of his high school Latin class,
then thought of English too and Bryon's Julia.
    Since Goldin never let an item pass,
he parsed this phrase he thought belonged to Sheba.
    It would have been insensitive and crass,
and more than Goldin's moral sense could bear,
to leave unanswered what was meant by fair.

For Goldin it was clear, the key was *but.*
    Why was she black *but* comely?
She was of ancient stock and not a slut —
    he conjured fair, its etymology —
yet she was black, and always racist cant
    gave little credence to non-white, and barely.
Now, English uses fair as meaning white —
confusing color and pleasant to the sight.

While thinking, Goldin swelled into a lion —
    imagined her delicious, dusky body —
and in his head arose a hungry dragon
    that also taunted him with what seemed tawdry —
why when one lusts for flesh, one seems to bargain
    with what the devil asks, writes history
in light of who one is, his nation's views,
that in this case was translated from the Jews.

The Phone Call

Goldin slipped a quarter in the slot,
listened. Pressed the seven-digit number
of his home and waited. Four rings and then:
"I'm sorry I'm not here to take your call,
please leave a number or call back."
He froze, waited for the beep.
"Ugh, Helen, this is Frank. I've missed you.
Hudspeth urged me to call. We need
to talk. I've been keeping everything inside.
I've had visions, night sweats. Sometimes
I hear your voice. Consider coming soon.
I know you're mad as hell. But what could I do?
It's all mixed up: Honshu, the time
she raised her skirts and winked, the phone
booth in Osaka, Yeager's isomers, IR spectra,
enzymes. I'm sorry I'm running on. Please call.
How are you? I've thought of Mexico. It's cheap.
They need biochemists. I need you.
Consider Mexico. Great hats! I love you. *Llamame.*

(   )

Goldin struggled with the importance of parentheses—
it seemed to him that everything he sought
or wanted to remember was contained,
not in the cement conduits of narrative thought,
but in stands of scrubby willow in parentheses.
Those asides that were not asides at all, those
small patches with little shade and the illusion of a stream,
in the nests of birds that sought shelter there,
avoided the scathing heat and at dusk flocked to a horizon
that Goldin looked to and from which he hoped
some direction would make itself known.
Eddies of dry air funneled up around the trees—
dust, detritus, debris, spicules, spores, and splotches—
fragments of content that were each a disassembled essence,
that caught bits of color as they rose in the light.
It was here in this light that Goldin looked
into the disorienting whirls in which order can be glimpsed.

Goldin Meditates on Providence

At the Tower of Babel, petitions—
each group claims the language of suffering.

At the well, accusations—
someone has poisoned the sheep.

Will no one come forward—
Who will take up the cudgel of radiance?

FROM

Remnant

(2002)

Jewstone

The Maker of Walls in Krakow
has ordered a wall for the city —
Pan Foreman, ready your plans,
your workmen and masons,
contact a purveyor of stone.
What have you got, purveyor of stone?
Sandstone that's soft and won't last,
and limestone and jewstone and granite.
Jewstone, purveyor, what's that?
Gravestone we sell for construction.
Which is the cheapest, purveyor of stone?
The jewstone's a bargain and local.
In no time flat you can have it.
Not to worry about its quarry.

The consignment delivered, the masons begin.
Convenient, the size of this jewstone.
Each rests on the next as if cut for this purpose.
This jewstone is perfect for walls, says Pan Foreman.
The task half-completed, the Maker stops by.
Pan Foreman, what can you show me?
Be lightning quick with your tour.
I have tea with a lady at four.
Here is the site, Lord Maker,
what do you think of our wall?
Too boring, too bland, he decrees.
Mark this place with its source.
Turn some gravestones face out
so that everyone knows
what went into the wall.

Today in Krakow
when shoppers or students pass by,
does anyone wonder
at the wall's Hebrew script —
Who is this Maker of Walls?
Is he the King of Glory?

Spicule

No sign jabbed
into the mound
says jew bone
and jew ash
from the jew camp.
But we know
that it cannot be
wop bone
or nigger ash
or spic bone
or chink ash
or mick bone
or wog ash
or jap bone
or honky ash
or salt
or crushed rock
or guano
or even gravel.
It must be
jew bone
and jew ash—
it has the mark
of systems engineering,
of the inevitable vector
from jew house
to jew train
to jew camp
to jew gas
to jew bone
and jew ash.

Commentary

Breathing is witness to air,
dissolution is witness to water.
Fire consumes. Earth keeps a vigil
before the dead are buried.
My witness is of another sort.
I keep watch over events I have not seen.
I have lost no family.
I was four in 1945.
My credentials are raising children
and doing research in Houston and St. Louis.
What am I, if I do not stand on one leg
and attempt a commentary?

Suitcase

Five-kilo life,
I am permitted to pack five kilos.
Clean underwear
a picture of my parents
our wedding picture
one of our children
toilet articles
two shirts
trousers
socks
father's gold watch
my medical instruments
a notebook
a pen.

Requiem

Rest in peace
it's a must
given the alternatives.
If you are dust in the air
rest in peace.
If you are dismembered
rotting in a ditch
rest in peace.
If you have been stuffed
down a well to drown
drink to life.
If you are decomposing by a road
seek wholeness.
More than rest in peace
seek reconstitution.
If you have been disemboweled or bludgeoned
rest in peace.
If you are lying in your blood in Prague
rest in peace.
If you have been gassed
and await the fire
rest in peace.
If you are ash
rest in peace.
Rest in peace
we need you to.

Black Forest Cake

chocolate batter
whipped cream
cherries
Martin Heidegger

Action Plan

The stars were gibbeted,
the moon sealed,
then hooded,
the wind put in irons,
the air disemboweled,
the cobblestones held hostage,
the rain incarcerated,
the songbirds gelded,
the sewers cinched down,
the vermin manacled,
the alleys cauterized,
the dust mites shackled.
Every brick was piked
until the Jews
were driven from this place.

Brown

Brown had no politics,
its palette was without guile —
chestnuts, withered leaves,
fields devoid of water,
November,
camouflage before winter —
its boots went unpolished.

Our Lady

Mary, did you ever visit Munich
and listen to the frenzy of the crowds?
Today I ask your intervention for the Jews.
Put distance between them
and the devil who eddies
the dust at the wheels headed east.
May your Son deliver them from the eagle's claw.
Give us the strength
to lower the semaphore and signal the brakeman.
I ask you in the name of decency
to implore Him on their behalf.
Do not let the devil win the day.
Ask Him to save those
whom He alone has preserved until now.

A Formal Proof of the Existence of the Holocaust

Pius the twelfth
and Roosevelt
didn't help.

Majdanek Window

Any knave could have crept
to the window lip
and used a sleeve to clean
the grim from the pane
or a knife to pry it open,
taken a chance and peered in.

Spring

Some morning fine beyond reason
when forsythia return to the fields
and my heart is small and grudging,
spittle will wheeze from my throat
and plaster the stubble of my beard.
Like a beggar, my heart will squat in parley
and wrangle with this vagrant over redbud,
argue about dogwood and crocus.

Motive

If I understood my motive for encryption,
for hiding behind the dead, it might allow
another self free reign — the stalker who
used a blade on the living before he dissected
the dead, the self now buried in the polite scientist
who dismembers genes. If I used a knife
to flake away the stone, it would expose
the raw wounds of my politics.
I might beat them at their game.
Somewhere in my brain, a sarcophagus cages
a flesh-eater who is devouring me from the inside
even as it preserves the relics of my past.

Dust

I have inhaled an alkali dust from the past,
taken it into myself, quicklime bitter.
I'm glad for the dust that coats
my lungs and prevents my speech.
I have no perspective beyond an acrid self,
no way to imagine mitigating circumstance.
There's no fair-minded analysis of bolt-action precision.
I am choking on a desiccated self
with the twentieth century as stand-in.
Dust might be a righteous gentile,
the pollen of lilies.

Amsterdam

Suddenly I bolt, running
for the bridge and the park beyond.
I am racing with all my might
and they lope along behind.
Fraülein, Fraülein, I hear one shout,
we have a surprise for you.
I'm in the park, running, gasping for breath.
Why have they not already caught me?
I hear them laughing.
I make it to the pavilion restaurant.
Before I can get inside,
one grabs me by my braids
and pulls me to the cobblestones.
Let's shoot the Jew girl now.
No, no I have a better plan,
and this one lifts my skirt with his rifle.
He drags me by my arm
into the restaurant and shouts,
Raus, raus, everybody out.
My back burns from the stones.
Let's see, one says and claws at my panties.
They yank my legs apart.
I scream. Don't, please don't.
A gun butt smacks my jaw.
The pain shoots to my ear.
I taste blood and broken teeth.
I cannot speak.
His pants are down,
his weight is on me,
I burn inside as if he took
a metal file to my innards.
I pray I'll pass out or die, but I don't.
More pain. I am wet with them and my blood.
Another. Oh, God, please, let this be over.
They leave me on the floor.
I am sobbing in a heap.
I do not know what to wish for.

Brain Function

Shale-hearted
light-blinded
grief-groveling
fact-gouged
gut-punched
shrapnel-cut
self-gnawed
mind-fucked,
I grapple with
the six-layered cortex
of myself
and its limbic goad.

A Still Life With Tire, Gravestone, and Boulders

needs a curator
to explain the method,
assure me that debris
is not strewn randomly,
and a geologist to put me
straight on boulders,
a chemist to analyze
the rubber of the tire,
the when and where
of its manufacture.
I push aside the rasp
of leaves and branches
and step through the trash.
My fingers touch the letters
on the gravestone's face—
eagerly, as if they were
the cheekbones of a woman.

Pledge

This is the last time I'm going to obsess about loss.

This is the last time I'm going to think about Jews dragged from Amsterdam, Salonika, Bucharest, Vilna, Riga, Prague, Vienna, Budapest, Berlin, Vichy France, Warsaw, Zagreb.

This it the last time I'm going to think about the exile of Nelly Sachs in Sweden.

This is the last time I'm going to remember the death of Paul Antschel and the suicide of Paul Celan.

This is the last time I'm going to think about Primo Levi.

This is the last time I'm going to imagine Bruno Schultz murdered by the Nazis.

This is the last time I'm going to reconstruct the lives of Jewish pharmacists and accountants, tailors, mathematicians, dressmakers, shopkeepers, housewives, professors, doctors, lawyers, poets, musicians, intellectuals, peddlers, traders, rag pickers, butchers, artisans, chemists, painters, and merchants during the Third Reich.

This is the last time I'm going to obsess about the deaths of Jewish children.

This is the last time I'm going to try to figure out what moves people to evil.

This is the last time I'm going to think about how fucking lucky I am and how many other Michael Liebermans were gassed or shot or strangled or bludgeoned.

This is the last time I'm going to imagine that winter predicts spring, that symbols of innocence mean innocence exists, that the fall can be splendid and prelude to a winter of quiet regeneration.

This is the last time I'm going to obsess about the beauty of flowers or honeydew or love or my children or family or loss.

This is the last time I'm going to think about grace and decency.

This is the last time I'm going to think about the Holocaust until tomorrow morning when I get up at four to read and do whatever it is that I am doing.

Time to Depart

With ice storms the issue is time.
Often in Houston or St. Louis
the ice comes as rain, so that
over hours there is an accretion
of weight, lamination after lamination
as the water freezes on the branches,
glistening even on nights
when the moon is down.
The gradual accumulation of scale
on the limbs until their tensile strength
gives way, molecules of wood fatigue,
and the branches sagging a little
and a little more, then more,
and gaining momentum lurching
toward the ground and snapping.
This is how death blossoms
on trees during storms like these.
This is how the physics of water
and mechanical force provide
time to prepare, to mourn, to depart.
Grace is a long good-bye,
a final look at the lasting beauty of the world.

Polish Poets

for Adam Zagajewski

I looked at Europe in the thirties and forties,
a vast territory I cannot enter,
a terrain you have mapped with fierce righteousness —
you sought out Rabbi Nachman of Brachlaw for advice,
but had no way to find him in the ashes.

Rabbi, are my words anything more than a fable of a fable?
Would your great grandfather in Vilna
or your student Zbigniew in Warsaw
raise a single shovel of earth in response?

My summary from this side of the Atlantic has failed.
As to the topology of suffering, I know nothing.
I cannot even smell the lindens
or feel the hexagonal tiles under my feet.

I ask the god of small poets to take pity on the Duchy of Lieberman
where I imprison my deceptions and hatreds.
Polish poets, release me,
come into my Duchy with fistfuls of poems.
Bless my meager lands and cities.
Teach me the gravity of earth and sky.

May a self-righting gyroscope inhabit me and guide me.
May I smell the lilacs of my parents' yard.
Polish poets, help me navigate the Vistula
that flows from Houston to St. Louis to Pittsburgh.

FROM

Far-From-Equilibrium Conditions

(2007)

Gratitude

I burned the crocuses when they danced naked in gray New Haven —
and after in Pittsburgh and St. Louis. I sat next to no one,
hoarded the oysterettes at my kitchen table in the tired light.
Only once or twice have I allowed myself to teem beyond the ordinary.
And now in this jowled abundance I stumble and dance.
Even if the gloom remain, I am glad for any sun that should rise —
pushed up by her own design or otherwise.
I cling to the tiny strawberries in the wild meadows of certain hearts.
I am the heartworm of those hearts, no more, and I am grateful.

Through My Study Window

If a shock of bamboo go
it be silently so
and if it move through me
may its move be slow —
this on days when the wind
says no to stirring willed or wished.

Meditation on West Gray

Stay with it, I say to myself.
    Get with the program and stay with it.

Li Bai is drunk in a boat on the Yangtze.
    The dam has flooded the river to a stagnant lake.
    Li Bai floats in the current of memory.

Don't go there.
    Stay on West Gray, keep walking.

The marquee of the River Oaks Three is a throw back to the 50s.
    Lots of high-minded films now. Soft focus.
    Hang in there, *El lenguaje del cine es universal.*

I suppose so, like the language of love, like the language of hope,
    like the language of drink, despair . . .
    like Chinese, one text and different sounds.

Go next door, the Epicure serves pastries in three languages —
    consider learning Persian, consider Darius the Great, consider Rumi.
    The language of hunger, the language of conquest, the
        language of . . .

Paco, my barber, will tell me.
    What's it like, Paco, to grow up gay in Monterrey?
    What's your take on the PRI and Vicente Fox?

Stay on West Gray I repeat to myself.
    Walgreens has it, you can get it there —
    a simple pill for what ails you.

Stop at the dry cleaners —
    he who steals your shirt may steal you soul.
    Consider the soul and neurochemistry —
    Essie has no interest in this delirium,
    she decides to hassle me over my lost ticket.

Modest illumination may accrue along this promenade.
  Stay with it, stay on West Gray.

Ignore the sunset, conjecture without fact is an inferno.
  Think about Dante, himself an inferno, a score-settler.
  Consider learning Italian.

Take instruction.
  God knows, take instruction. Horace matters.
  Stop at Kroger's, buy a knockoff of a national brand.
  Consider a poem, a poem for Dante or Rumi or Horace.
  For the moon Li Bai could not embrace.

Insufficient Sufis

Of course they're insufficient,
along with the postal service,
plumbers, doctors, the internet.
Perhaps you were thinking
that because they are holy
or poets or whirl like the wind
when provoked, there would be
something more, a vision,
a levitation, or perfect silence.
Not so. When you get
one of these fellows going
its gab, gab, gab. They drag
out one of the old books,
and let you have it for hours
without end — the world
as they see it. Or answers
to questions no one's asked.
They've never had to deal with merit badges
or an oil change. Try to imagine
a Sufi with a lawnmower. Of course,
they're insufficient for our needs,
they've never been here or done this.
I try to see the world as they see it —
to imagine redemption
beyond the next trash pickup,
salvation beyond direct deposit.
In the blinding sun I want
to expose myself to radiance
and be a little insufficient too.

Longing for Brick and HardiePlank

He noses the plumeria this morning
trying to distinguish among vanillas.
Checks out the stenciled addresses
on the curbs, anchoring himself
to the here of August in Houston,
hoping to provide a permanence
that the shimmering heat
will not carry up and away.
He wants to hug the trash receptacles
to countervail lift with heft,
the ugly ascension
that would force him to dwell
in the fragrance of another world.
He is reassured by contact—
the uneven pavement holds him,
proof of the ordinary imperfection he craves,
now, after angioplasty and stent
have made ascension not a dream,
but a terrible alternative to brick and HardiePlank,
the rain coming through the trees
and striking the windowpanes.

Conjecture

The future has no moving parts.
Schools of engineering will cease to exist,
docents will shred all evidence of pistons,
longing will hiss into space through a frozen valve.
Someone will silence song,
middle C will be a trace on a screen,
microcircuits will be unnecessary,
music will hemorrhage and die.
The heart's lub-dub will dwindle,
tenderness will persist in binary code,
love will vibrate like atoms in the gruel of space,
we will wonder why song existed,
kisses will be a remembered fiction,
touch will be something that was.
The torque of nothingness will ratchet us down.

Waiting for You at Lake Morena

for Zachary Andrew Wingman Lieberman (b. Aug 23, 2007)

The cottonwoods cling bitterly to the alkali at Lake Morena
and I wait for you.

There are miners trapped in Utah and an earthquake in Peru
and I wait for you.

Six-hundred die in floods in North Korea and others here
and I wait for you.

Not that you can redistribute forces, change the tides, or raise the dead
but I wait for you.

You will not reverse offenses we have given to this planet
but I wait for you.

I wait for your debut, instructor of the flawed heart — and flawed as well
yet you must do.

And still the cottonwoods cling bitterly to the alkali at Lake Morena
and I wait for you.

You will not move them to oak and hickory and then to beech
that is too much for you to do.

Yet I wait, little gurgler, giver of life, alien voyager from within us,
I wait for you to do — and do and do.

Messenger RNA

What do we do with a drunken sailor,
the little fella at the bar who says
watch out for your genome, the poisonous
glitches that spell doom in your forties
or death in your fifties? Give him
another drink and he'll talk gibberish,
sober him up and he'll have you
on a high fiber diet. No sense in piping
up the band, he's bleary-eyed, no chance
he's going to dance or tell you more.
No wonder he's drinking in the bar,
he's been sent to deliver a message
that won't be well received. Spare us,
bounce this treacherous Phaedippas
before he tells us more.

Port of Call

Freighted with antiquities
and crates of modern work
the Menil steams into our lives
glad tidings in its wake.
From its deck Magritte
is calling our name.

The Otherness

I wage a savage fight against insomnia,
even as I struggle to salvage the night,
to dive down beneath the darkness
and haul the unseen to the surface.
I listen to the hollow blow of a train
headed south across San Felipe.
Someone's mouser screeches at its prey.
The dog next door yaps blindly at another,
his point not altogether clear.
This ordinary tryst distracts me until
supplanted by another—a truck, its engine
straining to lift a dumpster from a parking lot,
a clanking virtue in the December chill.
More. Tire-squeal along West Gray,
the raucous snort of a drunk.
Another blow, the forced hot air
of the furnace obliterates this world.
I listen for some clue
while hibiscus roots push into resistant clay,
our neighbor's Chinese elm sheds
its leaves into my awareness, my wife
sleeps in a good marriage. I strain to hear
this world, the one that burgeons
with sounds unheard, unknown, unheeded.

Foreplay

Then there was the other one,
the one interested in Kierkegaard
who would solemnly engage me.
I didn't know a thing about Kierkegaard
and so I would parry with John Stuart Mill,
hoping that would move love along.
Which it didn't.

Instruction

Three things, he said, a man should do
before he dies — see *The Magic Flute*,
savor an artichoke, make love to a beautiful woman.
Still I am not ready. The poets of the Tang Dynasty,
what about them — those thousands whom
we barely remember? Was it enough to drink
rice wine and make love under the thunderheads?

Weather

for Susan

There is a snapshot,
    taken I think at Whittemore,
        in St. Louis, the occasion

David and Brenda's wedding
    from which you are absent—
        your mother,

younger than we are now,
    looks out next to me
        and to the side are both

our boys, almost toddlers.
    What would your absence
        be like?

      ♦

The only thing I remember
    distinctly from that day
        is flowers

not the wedding bouquet
    or those arranged on the tables,
        but catalpa

in the backyard blooming—
    big and generous clusters,
        the delicacy of each

lost in the massing of the whole.
    So much like you
        (how unsuited is the rose).

◆

In Houston, flowers
        even in robustness
                are not facsimile of you.

It is the weather
        I need.
                The splendid turbulence

that tumbles out of
        thirty thousand feet
                in dark festoons and pours

the contents of the world
        on top of us.
                Which is not

to dwell on the darkness
        in you, but to say
                the force of your love

is natural and grand
        and finds its way down to earth.
                The intimidating rains

of these clouds nourish all flowers
        that grow here
                that survive the weather's onslaught.

There is a danger in this power,
        but you have
                managed to control it.

        ◆

The weather
        is disorienting here.
                No winter to speak of,

and many years
    the spring is summer, and summer
        an infernal time

when the metabolism withers,
    cicadas quit early
        and one hibernates till fall.

   ◆

Fall is confounding
    for its mildness that predicts
        a colder phase in which

some flowers prosper,
    but is not by any stretch
        a summer.

I can't compare thee
    to a summer's day,
        they don't exist in Houston.

I must choose particulate weather
    like thunderheads to engage
        your passion

that feels to me
    colossal.
        And torrential rains,

here as fierce as anything
    in the tropics,
        that expose the seams of the land,

then give way to mildness.
    How else but weather
        to capture you? The generosity

that rain brings to the soil —
        rain that
                rejuvenates the sea —

not its erosive power
        but what fills us
                down to our last cell.

Whatever dryness
        is in me, you have
                washed out to sea.

◆

Look at any weather map —
        at the isotherms and isobars,
                those lines of constant

temperature and pressure, and you
        will believe we understand
                squalls and hurricanes,

that the scientist's imagination
        has put to rest
                the randomness of process,

that chaos theory has no role,
        that everything is in order.
                That's how a meteorologist,

would see it —
        all causes may
                be understood by rational analysis.

Yet we know such maps
        are fictions, at best approximations,
                that no one, at least

not now, can predict
    what moisture off the Gulf
        will do when it collides

with cool air moving south.
    I concede that in a general way
        we know we're in for rain.

But isn't it like a kiss? — there are
    kisses and then there are kisses.
        So one can never tell

about the rain in Houston.
    We know
        every so often there will be

a hurricane or something worse,
    a storm with a benign name
        like Allison that will

stagger us. That's the joy
    in your love — you never fail
        to stagger me, your kisses

blow off the sea with a strength
    and subtlety that leave
        the weather wanting.

No man has a right
    to so much. (I know that
        few men have it).

Anyone with a kite
    and patience can draw
        lightning from the sky.

But how many have a shot
    at our electrifying joy
        when we make love?

We know with precision
      how one air mass
            rubs against another

to transfer electrons
      to create capacitance and discharge
            and make sparks fly.

      ♦

But how is it that
      you and I
            lacking every instrument

have the means
      to incinerate the sky
            and leave it blue?

How is it that in perfect weather
      this act plays out
            as love and not release?

This chemistry is still a mystery,
      of course we know
            about tactility,

afferent neurons to the brain,
      the rush of hormones,
            but these explanations

of human lightning
      leave us cold
            and humdrum.

You've made a marriage
      of explaining this to me
            who often gets it wrong.

If I'm condemned
>to be your student always,
>>well, good that I fancy the teacher.

♦

The humidity of September
>is a postscript
>>a coda whose ink

is smeared by the heat
>as it tries to reach
>>out into the midst

of us, into the hugeness
>of our love
>>and swamp it, as the sea

might overwhelm fish,
>mollusk, crustacean, kelp
>>and cede to plankton.

Hard to think,
>my love, that our love
>>is plankton love,

the moving loam
>of the sea,
>>its landless soil

churned by the wind, exposed,
>common, abundant
>>and uniquely ours.

Obadiah in Love

Obadiah took a stab at prophecy —
just a snippet wedged among the others,
five minutes of predicting doom. Nothing more.
Did he dismiss this voice in favor of the world?
He might have farmed or traded dates and raisins,
a middle man, perhaps a trafficker, a profiteer.
Did he find love with his wife or was he an alley cat
or gay or lacking in desire? Can a prophet cheat
in love? What do prophets do when madness
dies and they are free of visions? Buy tangerines
from vendors in the streets, umbrellas? Could he
imagine grace or how sex might ripen into love?

Leaving Pittsburgh

I've been leaving every day
for forty years — the streetcars,
Panther Hollow, Roy Jones' lips
cracked from playing trumpet,
the day school that doused me
with chemistry and set me afire,
its hymnal, Latin, teen-age breasts.
I'm leaving Pittsburgh, headed out,
everything I own in the back seat,
leaving what's absent, what sits
on the cracked curbs, the acrid air
clutching at me, the midden of Pittsburgh,
the ailanthus trees and locusts,
the infernal gray of the sky,
the rose climbing cream-colored
against the kitchen window,
lilacs, my skin,
I'm leaving Pittsburgh intact,
never leaving it behind.

The Jack Man

At Keystone Box, Herbie
worked the pump jack,
a long-armed, levered hydraulic
that hoisted skids and pallets
he'd drag off to trucks
bound for Brockway Grass
or Ford City's bottling plant.
His job was to keep up,
keep the skids a coming,
and the workers humming,
not to let the line slow,
since this was piece work,
and they were bonused by the speed
they fed the cardboard in
and he swept the bundled cartons
truckward to the loading dock.

He wedged a wad between his gum
and cheek. Silence. No word passed
between him and the others. Wild-eyed,
he leaned on the long-stemmed handle
that once had claimed Don Wrobel's
teeth when something slipped
and it whipped through its arc.
The only flick of life was Herbie's
Adam's apple. He waited for a crew
to top off a load and motion him.

Don't think of the grit of Pittsburgh
or the lives as gray as the days.
Try to imagine the Serengeti,
Herbie haunched at the ready
eyeing the hyenas that fed him,
the lionesses that serviced him,
or a man in a denim shirt and jeans
on furlough from Western Psych
with a fistful of pills and knuckles
so clenched he could not take them.
May God preserve him — and all
the hapless jack men moving
this world forward on its skids.

Coaxing the Muse

Sometimes she is arthritic and could use
a boost, a tonic, something to get the juices going.
I've seen muses get stubborn, sulk in a corner
and refuse to help. They toss their sultry locks
and give you that get-stuffed-buddy look.
Just when you're ready to pickup your bag
and head for the park — you've got the idea
you'll watch a game of chess and write a bit —
she gives you that tough-broad look, digs in her heels
and says she aches and wants to stop for tea.

It's not supposed to work this way I tell her.
You're my muse, you've got obligations.
Inspiration's hard work. Get with the program.
Get real. I can see I'm having no effect.
Before I turn muse-beater, I gig her —
if you think you want another job,
you're going to need a reference.
If you don't get off your fat you-know-what
and help, I don't know what I'm going to write.
She levels her eyes at me as if to say: I'm tired,
I'm not sure I want to work much longer,
I've got some money socked away, and what
with social security and all, I'll manage.
Besides, musing's work for younger chicks.

Navicular

January, 2005

The small bones of the hand
are an archipelago of fear
that grasp at the splintered wood
as it slips between the fingers.
Beneath the sea is sinew,
molten beyond our ken. Above it
indifferent gulls lunge at the arcs
of fish who care nothing for sulfur or pumice.
Beyond the torso of Asia
the krill that crest with the waves
ignore our white-knuckle lives,
spill with the churn of the sea
to be swallowed by their own cetacean world.
From the shoals of our routine
gratitude erupts in slow motion.
We find a pen, write a check,
put the kettle on to boil,
make a cup of tea,
and sit at the kitchen table,
thankful for taxes and partisan bickering.

Gloss

Chilean Spring

Santiago—Saint Iago—
Fire in the branches
of the cherry trees.
Wet grass under my feet.

The North

Antofagasta, dry as a liar's mouth.
Calama whispers nothing.
San Pedro de Atacama,
sultan's eunuch, guards
the Valley of the Moon—
grit and bone.

The South,

that austral courtesan—
slick as an ad for trout
in an outdoor magazine.

Isla Negra

Neruda wrote a patter song with his life in this house—
the rooms are filled with shells, maidenheads, butterflies
and moths, mounted beetles and cockroaches, African masks
(we're told he never visited, gifts from friends), a trophy stove,
a bust of Jenny Lind, a papier maché horse from childhood,
a spyglass, writing desks (four, one made from the driftwood
door of a ship's cabin), a bed where he and Matilde slept,
pictures of Baudelaire, Whitman, Poe, Balzac, García Lorca,
Whitman again, closets with his clothes, memorabilia
from Burma, Ceylon, Jakarta, samples of his hand writing.
The table is set, a chair marked with a signifying place mat
for the captain of this Pacific trader, this silent house,
chockablock with everything but words. Out a window
beyond his grave, the sea in three-quarters view,
a cowlick of waves around the black rocks in the breakers.

String Theory

About one's dispatch there is no informed consent.
I will be assigned as nothing.
May it be a significant nothing,
a nothing to be proud of—
the leaf stripped clean to its veins
or just the mandible-hoisted green itself
or its chlorophyll, stomach-cleared,
enzyme-sheared to molecules,
the bleary wavelets of our universe
adrift in a universe of universes.

Not for Polish Poets Only

1.

For now, goodbye to Krakow
and the instruments of Canon Copernik,
the astrolabium from Cordova and the sextant of doubt.
Goodbye, rectors in your robes
and poets watering geraniums and waiting for a sign,
pigeons on the square, goodbye —
any biology student can inform on you.
Goodbye to Saint Mary's and your discarded leaflets
and to the bugler explained therein,
to good King Jagiello who continues
at this very moment to prevail against the Teutons
and the little restaurant behind him
where we ate pirogues and drank beer.

Goodbye to the phlox, hydrangea and willows —
sentries on the road to Auschwitz, a set with no actors.
We need a read through of what happened,
a handful of violets for each speaker at the end.
Goodbye to those events that never happened,
much more distant than Grunwald.
Jagiello lives, Copernik struggles, the rain
dissolves the face of the stones in the square.

2.

The oldest square in Central Europe
was revived in 1989. I do a little foxtrot there,
a shuffle for the uncertainty of progress,
the net, the fax and email. I hover over coffee
listening for microwaves, scanning the infrared
for a sign, expecting a message in regal ultraviolet.
At this moment not even ouzo could make me snake
between the tables in praise of Aphrodite.

I forgive those who carved the Jew musicians in the Cloth Hall—
after all, a fella's got to make a living,
all cathedrals, churches, chapels, and the parades
of gray habits, priests with guitars and school children
singing patriotic songs that swell the streets—I must let this be,
be something else, not Munich in 1933.
I forgive all tests of faith, all creeds,
but not the banishment of doubt.
I forgive not only because of my friends the Polish poets—
they can do nothing if a man pumps gas
or a woman buys a blouse or returns it to the shelf.
I forgive, not for the Polish sun,
but for the earth that revolves around it.

FROM

Bonfire of the Verities

(2013)

The Color of God's Eyes

Spinoza, God-intoxicated lens grinder,
knows the color of God's eyes, though
he chooses not to say, to cloud the issue
over like a cataract, to force us to contemplate
a face-to-face encounter with the darkness.
When we had our icons it was easier—
we could avert our eyes from his with confidence.
There was a heaven and a hell to burn in,
a place to pasture sheep. Refuge.
Like the patriarchs Spinoza has come
face to face with God. In good conscience
he cannot reveal their color. The brave man
chooses to be cast out and shunned
rather than sow discord with his doubt.
God, he thinks, has no eye, unless
it is the eye of the storm—the one we swirl
and swill in the taverns of our contemplation,
waiting for this Dutch Jacob to return
from his encounter, declare the contest
a draw and tell us that to be released
to life again, he has had to sign
a nondisclosure agreement, that all
he is permitted to say is that God,
who has one evil eye and one good one,
is the moving force of the universe.

Sphinx Moth

A sphinx moth sleeps under a light at the bus terminal.
All dressed up and no place to go.
All dressed up and everyplace to go.
A sphinx moth feeds at the honeysuckle,
sleeps in the night, waits for a call on his cell phone
or someone to come by with a question.
Not much you can't find on an iPhone these days.
One evening a girl does come by.
She tries out a conjecture on the drowsy moth:
The illuminated mysterious is the moth
and the moth is the word
and the word is the raptor
which hunts in the darkness,
solders the sequined light in place,
outlines and decorates the formless surface—
in the end what is fashioned
is only a beginning, as at every instant
of a journey another is beginning.
There are as many journeys as points on a line—
as many lines and lines of thought
as there are points and points of departure.
Look, the moth says, I've spent a lot of time
hanging out at the bus terminal. And sleeping.
You give me too much credit.

Specific Gravity

The density of a substance
relative to that of water or air.

Specific gravity is not specific,
not at all—at this moment
rosemary grows in our kitchen.
It measures one thing relative
to another—to light or drought
to sun and nutrients, perhaps to love,
or what the final meaning of fragrance is—
and in the bargain assures us
there is no final meaning.

Yet all the while we know
things finally mean—wars mean,
desecrations mean. Every incursion
has a specific gravity at every
check point in every parched land.

Gravity is always specific—
it is June, 1940 and the Germans
are advancing everywhere
and you are nine and running
with your family and escape
to X where they only have food
to feed themselves and you watch
your father swell and starve to death.
Or Hungary in 1956 or Prague Spring,
Arab Spring, Pinochet, the Towers.

(Gettysburg, Leningrad, Dachau—
the list is too long for a poem, a book, a library.)
The moisture of the spirit is relative
like a kiss, like humidity.
The world is full of specific gravities—

your four-year-old has cancer
of both eyes and doctors can save
his life but not his sight.
Your mother's Alzheimer's disease
that is yours as well as hers.

Earth has specific gravity, fire does.
Together they might be a consuming,
inelastic darkness—or a shelter.
Gravity is always specific as when
you get laid off in Detroit when your line
closes and your benefits run out,
and you are fifty-seven in January
with no heat. No one needs janitors
to sweep up broken glass and the leaves
the bitter wind pushes through the windows.

The number of specific gravities
in each heart grows at every second,
expands faster than the universe—
the specific gravity of connection,
of dissolution. Of stone or dust.
How many specific gravities of love
can we count—or grief or loss?
Tears have a specific gravity of one
against which everything else is measured.

The universe expands, our lives
drift, children learn to count
and what they can count on.
Conjecture joins things together,
sometimes absurdly, sometimes not.
You can almost be sure all gravity
is specific until the final freezing
of water in our landscape.

The Reason for Flowers

Each fall in Houston I'm bullish on flowers.
I never sell them short. I hunt bargains
like a Wall Street trader, values with an upside
that will shine in the winter darkness,
sound stock with growth potential,
impervious to cranky winds and intrusive frosts.
In a down market traders hedge.
I pass on Transvaal daisies.
Petunias will fade like a floozy at a truck stop.
I'll earn a little profit with begonias,
take a mild risk with impatiens.
In my yard, which swings hysterically between sun and shade,
I'll place a bet on sweet alyssum,
nothing elaborate, just a few pots
in the sun next to the warmth of the house.
Some dark morning three months hence
I'll get down on my knees, push my snoot
into those pots and breathe in the deep feminine—
 which is the only reason for flowers.

Notes Towards a Theology of Doubt

For the fiftieth reunion, Shady Side Academy
class of 1959. *Fide Semper Vincere* is the school motto.

1.
"Trust in God and keep your powder dry"
is a Cromwell quote we might apply
in place of *Fide Semper Vincere*.
I'll raise a glass of cold Vouvray
or a Bud or mug of Guinness Stout
to all of those who favor doubt.
I count myself among the pack
that sees faith riding on doubt's back.

2.
In the event of my death
remember it is timely.
Who can live, abundantly
or otherwise, beyond
what neutral circumstance permits?

3.
A torrential rain off the Gulf
has puddled in my driveway.
Mare nostrum, I remember —
the Romans owned it all, or everything
they thought worth owning. I am,
I think, master of a disappearing pond.

4.
I am one who ignores
advice and could succumb
to gluttony if the Lord
would grant me petit fours,
but if he plays the maverick
and offers up Italian —
sweet Lord, think linguine with clams —
I'll be pleased to suffer garlic.

5.
I am death's customer,
sure I want to purchase nothing
in his kiosk of rancid wares —
I ask for a store credit, I tell him
I'll wait for the new lines in the spring.

6.
What would you say to a wager —
a bet that somewhere between
Whole Foods and Kroger's
there are the hungry and the needy
and I am going to pass them by?

7.
Sun going down on Memorial Day,
and through the chain link fence —
oleander, the burl of a long dead
tree stuck in the links, persisting
like gristle between the teeth.

8.
Some days I walk flat-footed,
sometimes I shuffle or shamble,
or gimp — disguise my arrival,
hoping death will bar the door
and turn the bolt against my entry.

9.
Received wisdom at a gas station
on the card of a real estate broker —
Isaiah 32:18: And my people
shall dwell in a peaceable habitation.
Omitted are the street address and zip code.

10.
All roads lead to Rome
except the Tour de France
except the Ringstrasse,

that Ouroboros of faded modernity,
except the bridge to Toledo
except the Trail of Tears
except the road to Santiago de Compostela
except the autostrada to Firenze
from Rome which leads
like the others to our eking out
the yardage of our forward progress.

11.
A solitary wasp ignores
the blossoms of my vinca
and forages beneath the leaves.
What can her quest be
that commands my full attention?

12.
I must manage with the quotidian,
never accepting less, never waiting
at the bus stop of a shabby barrio
or in imagined savannas and open forests —
waiting for fineness to crystallize
into my life, never accepting imperatives.

13.
Who has agency in the hardscrabble
land of the spirit, unless it is
our impoverished selves, famished,
each of us, feral and lost,
in the iPhone marshes of the present?

14.
Civility in all things civil
is what we need, Jung thought.
Yet consider an assault on darkness,
the high barricade to be breached
with total disregard for form if we are
to return to a common discourse for our woes.

15.
I'll not disguise my lewdness
when it comes to flowers.
Earlier you glimpsed forsythia,
which makes me randy, crazy with lust.
Now I offer you six newly planted roses,
every thorn starved for water
in the inferno of a Houston summer.

16.
We live under the freeway of ourselves,
our urban shades our meager offering,
illuminated by trafficking in the only
squalid splendor we can know.

In This Poem I Predict the Coming of the Messiah

Set aside from each other like birch
and olive tree are the "I"s and "thou"s
that steal each other's lines
in a bad comedy skit. Who says,
Many are called and few are chosen, or
Called or not the gods are present?
We are the Torquemadas of ourselves—
who else can we be? We are
called out, found out by our torments.
What if one's calling
is not to come out but to wind
around the stylus of one's self,
spindled and waiting
to wring small miracles of doubt
from the latrine within?
Or to unwind, to wend toward
a black province after the sun
drops dead and mosquitoes suck
you dry of everything but
the pure discomfort of being?
Now you're talking Messiah.
(Don't think those uninvited gods
don't have their own problems
with gout and vermin. You are
not alone in gratitude for
strong coffee and the sunrise.)
To be self-piked, self-impaled
by one's innards, is unbearable.
A god has to do what a god has to do.
You wait in a dark cave for three days,
hoping the mystery will swaddle you,
the transcendent other will suffuse you,
and then you get the fuck out
before the roof caves in.

The Cloisters

We took the A train as instructed.
Of course they were old instructions,
and whatever it was he wanted us to do
in Harlem, we didn't. We had other plans
that morning, though by mistake
we got off at a hundred and ninth to ask.
Oh, you're way too early. Catch the next one
north—which is what we did.
Okay, I thought, this is okay
as we rattled amidst noise and sway
and determined Kindle readers.
I tried to imagine the way it was
for Trappist monks during the long,
silent winters of Northern France—
only the chanting and the wind
and the hope of God's voice.
I admit to guilt around the subject
of extreme submission. Such repose
for me is too much of a good thing.
Sometimes I need to escape the quiet,
though the subway felt like subjugation,
each of us trapped in jarring isolation.
I had no hope of losing myself like the man
across the car who squinted at a Bible.
I was glad when we left the racket and broke
out to the light—the Hudson far below,
still, on a windless day. A brief walk,
and once inside the gates, we faced a swell
of granite, bare and cleft, and everywhere
quarried through with pools of azaleas
and tulips that took us prisoner.

Tuesday Afternoon

In Memory of Jack Gilbert

We don't say much about him,
she smoking a cigarette and I
drinking black coffee from a mug,
both of us looking out on
the street below. Yet something
must be said. He can no longer
speak for himself. Tau protein
has tangled his thought and
plaques have destroyed his words.
Should we mention the girl
in the blue halter below,
or the tree busy being green?
Would that do it, bring back
the Aegean, the black sands
of Santorini or Thira
before the catastrophe—
or him before the slow devastation,
before he was left alone
in the ebb of his thoughts?

Grant's Atlas of Anatomy

My mother lived on fissured hills of fail,
a crumbling landscape I cannot guess,
on denuded ridges almost devoid of gods.
Then Eris in a final act of leaving eroded
her life to a moonscape of despair.
Strange animals rooted in that gravel-shale,
unparsable in their ordinary foraging.
I am certain once she was young and lithe,
but later if she danced, she danced alone
in those uncharted regions. Wild
does not describe that strangeness.
Then even the pilot light of her luster
was snuffed out, first turned down
by my father and later doused by booze
and loneliness. The girl in her burned
out long ago. I was blinded by the gloom—
in the fog-bound valleys I could not see
beyond the trailhead. I supposed I knew
the contour of her life from the detailed
map of gyri and sulci I had before me.
For too long I did not know that she was lost
among the ravaged proteins and exploded
vessels or imagine that an evil wind
had blown her out of her life into an abyss.
It is a sadness that before she died
I did not grasp her aloofness was coerced.

Narcissus, the Flower, and Then Some

The light off the sea is erratic
as it tacks across the surface,
subject to the whims of wind and current—
even Apollo is buffeted, lives
the helter-skelter life we all do
as he struggles to catch up,
install a more stable operating system
on his laptop for his traverse.
Enter Narcissus, the flower,
profuse behind a picket fence,
sequestered in a nearby yard—
he has no truck with failed delivery,
disdains incompetence which cannot plan ahead,
looks away like an untargeted missile
with no eye to the sun, no way—
no interest even—in tracking
that sun's arc. He locks in
on one of his stellate blossoms.
The blinding fragrance intoxicates us.
Now even the blind shall see.
We are prisoners of this tyranny,
captives of a warlock in white robes
(well-doused with cheap cologne)—
a klansman, who lures us away from the light.
Narcissus is a solar system of his own.
You cannot blindside this fellow,
he is the star of his own firmament—
the warder of his own presidio.

An Orange Tree in Autumn

Houston, Texas

This one stands well-sheltered north and west,
the oranges ripening slowly. Like poems
they survive in sundry pockets, in the corners
of yards, unattended, havened by rent houses,
tumble-downs and our own—not quite abandoned,
but feral, without intent, unruly intruders
in our landscape, each a miraculous thicket of promise
left fallow not by truancy or neglect
but by an incremental awareness that awards us being.

X in Winter

Some mornings in the dark corners
of yards in California the tiny
flowers open on the jade plants
and push aside their succulence.
Shelter me. I ignore wisteria today,
their hanging gardens of Babylon.
There is no communing with rosemary,
its ripe smell, its sapphire
emerging ahead of spring.
If you can spare the time away, set
aside the jostle of the everyday
and shelter me. You have no lushness
to unfold—each fleck of petal smaller
and less bold than the marring white fly
that will soon emerge and suck hibiscus dry.
Bougainvillea is a privileged harlot,
a tawdry, difficult, thorny bitch—but comely.
You sit alone on a ledge in a pot,
assimilating minerals and metabolizing
as if the wizardry of the commonplace
were nothing, a nod to the ordinary.
You are a presence inured to every
other event but being. Shelter me.

Conduit

I should not be surprised,
given the folly of rapture
on an ordinary morning like today,
that no one has come, the only
emissary the path itself covered
with well-worn bark and chips
fresh from a storm-downed beech
past the school to the playground.
Yet in that park I had hoped
to look down a length of pipe
into a promissory breach
and see my mother there, young,
as she was when my father
married her or when she suckled me.
A conduit—something concrete,
like those that enchant our children
or guide spent runoff to the sea—
might carry my mother back to me.
Only a fool petitioner would ask
a song or goddess—something rare—
to touch her body and guide it up
or imagine that she, ten years
dead, might climb out to me.
The choice instead must be to put
aside the fear, no, dread, and clamber
down love's trace to enter into her,
who, when I will allow, still suckles me
across this ancient space.

Certain Measures

I am the court Jew of my life,
the guest worker of my soul —
before the gods peck my liver out,
may I convert my truths to doubt.

Vigil

Houston Hospice
September 23, 2010

Hers is an ordinary life that cannot see
the gold amaryllis clinging to bloom
beyond the breezeway, a life no longer hydrated
by the rattle of tubes and lines, the ratchety
click of perverse machines that meter out
hope before a cracking dike. Soon death
will come up over the bayou and swamp her
with no promise of redemption,
no restitution for our loss —
as it is with ordinary lives.
One by one her synapses uncouple
leaving islands of sensate loss,
her dendrites retreat to the shoals,
and she is left adrift in the murk.
Last week, her face, a defiant rictus,
stared down the rising water.
Her eyes closed and the welling-up slid down.
I don't know — no one can see
into the souls of our ordinary lives
as we wait with her for death
to fledge up out of the bayou.
We urge you, make haste, she has slid
past outrage and fear. She waits. We wait.
May the force that animates the waters
draw them up soon and exert a healing tug.
Sweet undertow, our ordinary lives are ready.

Giacometti's Armature

Last day of the year
the fog has lifted
like a woman's skirt
revealing
her unshaved legs.
I wait for the sun
to dissolve this metaphor,
a view of the world,
I am unhappy to admit
as mine, admit
to this poem. Edgy,
addicted to radiance,
I want to edit out
the bland, the terrifying,
the black-dog presence,
write a comedy —
foxglove in the open woods,
lawns ending in hydrangea —
hide away burn victims,
those immolated by conviction,
exile fatigue, loneliness,
every affliction,
even lack of
concentration.
This poem
bears the shape
of Giacometti,
who accepted
the ugly
made it
serve beauty —
Giacometti,
whose
armatures
lance
preten-
sion,
en-
vy.

Souvenir of Provence

In the square at Gordes
the names cry out for reading.
Time has warped our memories
of the citizens and soldiers who died
in the world wars. They call
from the sewer of history —
the trenches, the gas and typhus,
the disembowelments, all those
who died alone in the mud,
which is to say most, ignored
or forgotten, present this afternoon
on the monument at Gordes.
The names go unnoticed. Perhaps
the light is too fierce for our gaze,
or life's needs too pressing.
Save one fished from the cloacal stream.
Joseph Bonfils died the granite
tells us "in occupation," a sprig
of Sephardic Jewry in the sun,
blooming in the rock, remembered
but unrecognized, a life struggling
to be known in the chaos
of our everyday concerns.
Who is the righteous one
who helped us siphon back
his name from the camps
and brought him to this moment?

Pulsatile

Circe is not circadian,
she is the ever-present—
always on the prowl—
born even before the gods
invented systole and diastole,
a pulseless heartthrob
who turns men to steers
and then to grief
with her blowsy ways.
Her wares are the come-on
of Prosecco and roses,
the come down
of roaches and fleas.
You invite yourself in
and she puts out your lights.
You find yourself in the trough
of a featureless landscape
where time is a fog,
each day a day in November,
stripped to your skivvies
in the muck with the others,
dimly aware of your nowhere.
(Here, sports scores don't matter,
you forgo the cheap booze
and the chips, the breath mints,
the latest news of the market.)
You are a castrated gladiator,
too weak to raise a sword.
What you retain is your hate
for your slough-mates
who vie for her hand.
You are sure she will return,
choose you alone,
ungeld you, make a man of you,
anoint you her consort.
Oh, how you long to be chattel,
a homunculus of the self

you were and nothing more.
You are not man enough
to know what to wish for—
the intervention of a god,
a Poseidon, a Zeus or a Thor,
a shave and a ferry ticket
across the still waters,
safe conduct to your own heartbeat,
the restoring balm of violent storms,
their bracing peaks and disheartening troughs.

In Praise of the Arts

Ein bisschen Titian
kindles frisson.

Remembering My Mother

Illuminated by black light,
my mother's life phosphoresced a sadness —

an imagined girlhood
eclipsed by her mother

pubescence wilted
by her shyness

ambition called to spoilage
by dyslexia

longings mashed down
in the blur of the thirties

fimbrial journeys unnourished
by my father

who in his dying bequeathed
her alcohol and pills.

Where are you now, coltish girl
who raised me to life?

Where will you be when molecules
vanish at the end of time?

After the Fall

Death blindsides you
with its lurking particulars.
You fail to notice
the macadam scraped away
on 53rd Street at the MOMA,
the raised manhole rim
that catches the toe
of your running shoe,
and you are suspended —
nowhere for an instant.
And there, without regard
to flaws or fame,
good deeds or bad behavior,
without judgment,
chance deals your hand.
Inside, on an upper floor
death sits patiently.
Otto Dix and George Grosz
catch the depravity of war
and the dark pool
beneath the streets of Weimar.
Schiele dies before
his nightmares come alive.

Defining Depression

There are rivers that must be crossed,
silt threatening particulate gold in a forbidding sun.
The far shore with its cobbled landing
offers nothing but what we leave behind.

Meditation for the Last Night of My Life

After translating some poems of Antonio Machado

Listen, if I die tonight, don't worry.
We saw a movie, had a meal,
grumbled and stopped for groceries.
What else is there except a clarity
I could cloud over with a poem?

FROM

The Houstiliad, An Iliad *for Houston*

(2015)

Achilles Kills Mestor and Abducts His Wife

from Book I: Riding in the park at dusk on an old BMW motorcycle,
Achilles and his white macaw Patroclus come upon Mestor and his
wife. After initial pleasantries, he eyes the man's Rolex.

The biker's big, well-muscled. He glints and glares,
then reaches down and hefts a tire iron.
　　"Hold on, the Rolex you can have, my wallet.
Whatever else you want. I beg you, please."
　　Her mouth is clotted, a knock-off of "The Scream."
　　"I beg you, leave my wife and I alone."
　　"I must. When people beg for mercy, none
should be forthcoming. Honor dies with begging."
　　"You're crazy, from some creepy movie. This
can't happen here. No way. We're leaving now."
　　Then fierce Patroclus rages in his face
and stills him upright — stopped dead in his tracks.
Achilles catches the Rolex arm, then brings
the tire iron smartly down and rips out
his cheek and jaw. A second blow midships
the temple spills his brains in creamy florets
and sucks him through the black hole of forever.

"Do it. Do it," Patroclus whistles. "Do it."
　　The Biker grabs the breasty woman, lifts
her, stuffs her in the sidecar. "Say one word,
you're dead." He holds Patroclus in one arm,
nape kisses him, speeds north, and kills his lights,
turns off a quiet Farm to Market road,
then lurches through the rutted dirt and cuts
the engine at a copse of oak and scrub.
　　"You scream, you die, that clear?" He binds her with
some bungee cords and laughs.

Achilles Refuses to Atone For His Crimes

from Book I: Achilles has killed Mestor and abducted, raped, and
murdered his wife. He appears to have gotten away with his crimes
but suffers momentary remorse, then tries to lay the blame on
Athena, his inner guide and mentor.

Remorse arrived like a summer of crows.
He shooed the birds as if they were the plague,
thought to recall the envoys, then banished them.
    Athena, commissure of my journey, you,
I longed for when I took that woman, raped her.
I only sought your counsel, your consortium.
Athena, you ignored me, so I had her.
Fate dealt me her, her death, my swag, escape.
Return and educate me — lead me out
of impulse, as I writhe naked in the slough.
He closed his eyes and sought the woman he
had known since second grade and always loved —
the women nested in him by his manhood,
that residue of fire trusted to him,
the boyish, gray-eyed goddess, virgin temptress
whose face and smile surged within him though
a thousand layers down. His psyche's keep
impeded her, not willing to accede
to Cronus' soul-submerging, evil sway,
as if to say, "Bend first to me, renounce
your unchecked rage and I will give you access
to the goddess. Now you cannot hear her."
A riptide of desire had swept him out
to sea, but she remained hard-wired in him,
offline but ready in his circuitry,
I won't atone, I won't. I know it's wrong
but you deserted me. I'm lost and still
search every pretty face for you, Athena,
commissure and journey — limbic you,
nebulous anchor of clarity, deceit.

Aphrodite Convinces Paris Alejandro to Meet Helen

from Book III: Paris Alejandro (Alex) wanders into his friend
Aphrodite's shop, Boutique Cythera, one morning when a burst
water main forces him to close his hair salon.

He looked at her, the sunlight in her hair,
the sea in his amygdala, his being
freighted with her beauty. He could smell
her sex as steamy as Cythera. An
inferno of desire seared him. *Just ask
her out. The crucible is yours to fire.*
    The goddess, knowing everything, had sensed
his mood, "You hitting on me, Alex? Come clean."
    "Is that so bad? I've always fancied you?"
I'm going to have a little fun with this,
thought Aphrodite. *It's my due as goddess.*
    "Well, yes and no. You know my reputation.
I'm with a guy a month and then it's over.
We're friends, let's keep it there, no more."
                 "Your face
is peerless. Acolyte kazoos should praise
your beauty! Then tambourines and trumpets. Tell me?"
    *Where does he get this crap? I bet he took
creative writing classes at UH.*
    "Very cute, but no, it's not a go.
We'd scrap and kill each other in a week.
But friends are friends—I'd like to help you find
a woman suitable for love." *But truth
be told, I'll sow a little mischief too,*
she thought. Then lewdness overtook her plans.
*"love" and "evil," are near anadromes.
I'll lead him on a bit and see what happens.*
"Again, it's love not marriage that you seek?"
He nodded. "I have a customer, a lass
of stabbing beauty, Helen, charming and
discreet, a woman restless in her marriage.

She's hinted that she's bored with Menelaus.
They're rich and live in River Oaks. Together,
her husband and his brother Agamemnon
hold vast reserves of oil around the world,
so money's not the issue. I'm sure of that.
The woman's tethered, ripe, and zesty—ready
for adventure. I'm never wrong. Trust me.
I think your playfulness and verve will draw
her out. Use the line about kazoos—
it's wacky, crisp, and quick, just right in tone
without an ooze of serious intent.
You'll see. Bizarre *bon mots* appeal to her.
At home she's in a prison of convention,
stifled by him. It's right, I promise. What say?"
     "Look, Dite, something guided me to you
this morning. Some force I can't explain and now
wants us to be a pair. Can you not feel
the current?"
           "Alex, poor boy, get real. We would
dismember one another in a heartbeat.
Yes, we could get it on, but keep it on?
Never. You have to trust me. Helen's right."
     "Dite, I'd hate to miss a chance with you.
You're wrong, I know you're wrong, so listen . . . "
                    "No,
no. Absolutely not. No, Alex, no."
     "You're one tough broad. . . . You win. . . . Uncle, tell me."
     "Look, Alex, I know my customers, and you,
my picky friend, will not be disappointed.
She's coming for a fitting later. I'll
direct the conversation cautiously
to love and probe her state. I'll try it out.
I'll warm her up and send her by your shop.
I promise you'll know what to do from there."
     She kissed him on the cheek and sent him packing.

Helen Leaves Her Husband Menelaus for Paris Alejandro

from Book V: Helen realizes Menelaus knows she is having an affair with someone and fears that he will physically harm her. Alex (Paris Alejandro) offers her shelter and suggests she move in with him. Caught by passion and fear and with only a twinge of guilt, she leaves.

She backed her Jaguar out and left that life
before eleven. Four years of marriage down
the tubes — the garden club, the lunches, and
drab afternoons of chick lit at her book club —
the heavy weight of Menelaus on her.
Behind her she left nothing. Did she feel
regret or shame, remorse or even grief?
Let's say that passion swept her forward so that
these questions never entered consciousness,
as if she'd left one frat boy for another.
Too bad for him, but he'll get over it.
Yet still a twinge of sadness stayed with her —
good girls did not betray their husbands. Did
an unseen moral stripe lay buried to freight
her leaving with an existential guilt?
Was her self-serving action in service to
her deepest Self? And how is this decided?

Was Menelaus to blame for her departure?
Of course he was no model of a man,
but neither was he evil. Jealous was
another matter. Was Othello evil?
Were both betrayed by primal, limbic fears?

But Helen? Helen knew the fault was hers
at least in part. She chose the easy path
instead of facing problems in her life.

Someone as bright as she had many options:
she could have worked at Rice or U of H,
or volunteered at the Jung Center
like Cassie. A PhD was not beyond
her skills. Or just plain worked in marketing
or sales. Is boredom license to break a marriage?
To ask forgiveness might have been first choice.
Of course divorce was not an option now
that she and Alex were screwing with abandon.

So what to make of Helen and her spouse?
Is blame or judgment something we can render?
Are memes a help or only parquet flooring?
Ditto norms and mores, moral values.
Is neural circuitry a certainty?
Is there a choice but living in the story?

Her leaving made no sense to Menelaus —
which is the understatement of our tale.
That night he found the note and called her folks.
Her mother said they hadn't seen her and weren't
expecting her. He knew at once and called
her cell, "I'm deeply sorry. I was wrong,
so please come home. I know that I was out
of line. Can we not talk this through, my love?
Come home to me."
         "Look, Menelaus, I'm not
returning now or ever. I was prisoner
to your life. I need to live, not die
of suffocation." She hung up on him.

Hector Kills Patroclus, the White Macaw

from Book XII: Earlier Achilles and Patroclus showed up at Hector's office and threatened him. In the process Patroclus, triggered by a bra and panties Achilles had trained him to respond to, strafes Hector tearing into his shoulder and lancing an ear. Hector swears revenge and plans to capture Achilles and kill Patroclus. Hector and Euphorbus arrive at Achilles' house one evening. Achilles is out, but they encounter Patroclus in the kitchen. His girlfriend's unfolded lingerie is on the counter. A struggle ensues in which dishes are broken. Patroclus has been knocked to the floor, but now, recovered, he flies at Hector.

[Renewed, Patroclus] tried to slash the Hammer
but crashed instead into the fridge. Then Hector
swung and hit the bird athwart, a blow
so smart it knocked Bird to the floor. He lunged,
went sprawling on the glass, and grabbed
the bird who bit him on the hand. He cursed,
but now he had a better purchase.
                              "Euphorbus,
quick, the rope." With one fist Hector snatched
the claws and bundled them. The other held
the body to the floor. That left the beak
to peck at him. Somehow he found a way
to make a slipknot of the cord, a noose,
and as he struggled to ensnare the neck,
the bird attacked his hand.
                              "You motherfuck,
you die."
             He fixed the noose and motioned back
Euphorbus, cinched it, and softball deft, he pitched
the bird aloft and slowly spun him. Slowly,
slowly. Just enough to choke a bit
and guide its course. At first it seemed the bird
was flying round and round, as if a child
were playing in the park, but as the speed

increased, the flapping ceased. The Hammer's face
was all sardonic grimace. Faster, he whirred
the bird apace. Euphorbus felt the wind.
They heard a snap and knew the task was done.
But faster, faster still, he spun the bird,
himself half-crazed, imagining Achilles
orbiting around him. Now Hector saw
the bras and panties on the table and felt
the shame of both attacks. A hateful rictus
beset his face which hid his gnawing wound.
He whipped Patroclus harder round the room.

"Stop it, Hector, stop, you're mad. It's just
a dead macaw, that's all," Euphorbus said.
        "I'll quit, but it's not over. Achilles loved
Patroclus, cherished him—much more than men
adore their dogs. Patroclus made him glow.
Note, I say 'made' not 'makes.' It's our advantage."
The bird lay wrung out at his feet. "Achilles
will want to bury him. Watch this. He'll not
get all of him, no way. I'll have my charm
from flesh, a lucky talisman, much better
than a rabbit's foot." He took a cleaver,
let out a yelp, and, thwack, he whacked through bone
and tendon at the "ankle," which left a claw
and tarsal trophy. Then he spit on him.
        "Achilles will not fail to notice how
the tendon is transected at the heel.
I'll take this to a taxidermist, have him
surmount the tip with silver, and wear the foot
looped through my belt and taunt Achilles. Each time
he sees me, he'll go mad with hate. Revenge,
 how sweet, when wronged by naked rage or Fate."

Menelaus and the Ajax Boys Retrieve Patroclus' Body

from Book XIII: Hector has dangled Patroclus' body along with a
Texian "Come and Take It" flag from a bridge over White Oak Bayou.

With Menelaus the others headed for
the bridge. Big Ajax Gross went first, ice pick
in hand and backed by Ajax Kurtz who waved
a sawed-off shotgun. They sprang and rushed the ruck,
the others right behind. The six defenders —
the Mexicans and Hector and Aeneas —
were caught off guard. Gross grabbed the flag and hooded
one, then kicked him in the groin, and tossed
him.
       "Come and take it," little Ajax cried
and fired a warning blast.
                           Big Ajax jammed
his pick into another's arm and floored
him with a cross. The other *vatos* ran.
Cowed Hector and Aeneas shrank — this Gross
was rapier fast and diamond hard. Kurtz fired
a second warning shot. Meriones
watched Menelaus hoist the body up,
then cut the stanchioned cord and cradled him,
and without pause he whisked Patroclus back.
That ugly rope, which trailed, the hangman's noose,
now scudded in their wake along the pavement
Resolve returned to Hector, who charged the two.
       "Come closer, and I'll turn your face to *salsa
roja*. If you doubt me, come." He stopped,
not sure of Kurtz's courage, "Despicable,
you useless turd, you chicken shit."
                                    Next Gross
let fly a martial throwing star, but Hector
adroitly dodged the whirr and cursed them both.
They turned, and racing for the cars, all four
arrived at once. Then Menelaus laid
Patroclus on a crimson carpet.

The Biker Kills the Hammer

from Book XIV: Athena counsels Achilles not to seek revenge for
the death of Patroclus, that killing Hector is not a path to a hero's
glory. He ignores the goddess, and after a beating up Hector's friend
Agenor and his buddies at Café Apollo, he comes upon Hector, who
turns and runs.

He lit out after him past tattoo shops,
boutiques and stores, four other coffee shops
around the block—a hippodrome of wheeze
and puff, though both were fit and strong. Three times
around the block they went. The patrons and
the gods and goddesses were stunned at Hector's
stamina and speed. Achilles raced
in vain. Then gray-eyed Fate, his friend, stepped up:
The Hammer tripped and sprawled. He landed at
a tarot reader's on a quiet street.
Achilles sprung full force, and leopard quick
he dragged him to his feet.
               "Now, Hector, stand.
Your death's at hand. You know as well as I
your fate. You killed the one I valued more
than any but Briseis, and for that
you will pay dearly."
               "Want to bet, Achilles?
I've got a Glock. Take stock and deal with that.
My finger's itching to recycle you.
I'll kill you fair and square. I have not doubt,
but I propose a pact whereby we each
agree to heroes' honors for the other
and the return of bodies to our kin.
For after all we both are warriors—
soldiers—and value custom, duty, honor."
        "I can't believe I'm hearing this abuse.
What's this? It's crap you speak, pure garbage, dreck,
the kind of shit you hear from fearful scum.

You are no more a soldier than was Judas.
Once I kill you—I promise that I will—
I'm going to hack you up and pack you up
in tidy plastic garbage bags with ties,
for you are garbage, *mierda*, pure and simple.
I'll drive your pieces north toward Navasota
and scatter you for feral hogs to eat.
You will be barbecue for swine post haste."

Cold fear filled Hector's eyes and paralyzed
his hands. The Glock stayed holster-stashed, pure schlock
against the Biker's rage at lost Patroclus.
It froze the Hammer to a mannequin:
stalagmite-still he stood. Out came the cord
the Hammer used.
        "Please don't, Achilles, I'll
do anything you ask."
        "Then bring Patroclus
back. Now. . . . What? No?"
        He flung the rope around
his neck—garroted him right there. It was
an execution—crude, effective, without
finesse. He cinched the rope as tight as he
was able. Agenor's bug-eyed features crossed
the Hammer's face. He twitched, went slack, and twitched
again. His ruddy face turned cordovan.
His tongue hung out and dribbled frothy slobber.
He crossed his eyes and peed his desert khakis.
A last reflexive jerk helped raise both hands,
which tried to loose Patroclus' cord. Life spent,
he slipped to vermicelli limp and died.

Athena Pulls the Plug on Achilles

from Book XV: Achilles has planned an elaborate, hero's funeral for Patroclus. Halfway through, Athena arrives. Exasperated by Achilles' madness, his lack of remorse, and his inability to recognize that Patroclus is only a bird, she demands that he submit to her and resolves the story.

    "What will become of my best friend Patroclus?"
    "Achilles, please, let go of all of it."
    "Not easy, he's a part of me, like you."
    "Not true, Achilles, he's a bird. You conjured
a comrade in arms. A bird, a motley bird."
    "And me, Athena, what will become of me?"
"I'm benching you. Beginning now, you'll sit
next season out."
              "I want to play. I want
prime time — and honor, women, dominance —
a feature story on Fox or CNN."
    "My friend, it's done for now. It is my way
or free agency. That's it. You choose.
This is the deal I offered many others:
I'll have control. You'll get the outward credit.
If not, you're on your own. Good luck adrift
in a wine-dark sea without a guide like me.
Take it. That's my advice. But you decide.
You want to spend eternity archived
in moldy tomes or live through me, Achilles?
With me, you'll live to fight another day.
Just trust me, it's nice work and you can get it."
"My dear Patroclus who art in Heaven,"
                            "Stop,
Achilles. Don't make it harder than it is.
Anima replacement therapy
is what you need to heal your subluxation.
We must reprogram every blessèd neuron
and superglue your psyche back together.

And you don't have a single guiding crone
of any sort. You need one for her wisdom.
I can't do all the heavy lifting. And what
about some shades of love not sullied by
the goddess from Cythera. I'll put out feelers
for Isolde, Heloise, and Ruth.
Let's set aside the gamy Greeks.
There's always too much downside risk with them.
We've got to get you off bewitching babes
and birds that rub your privates publicly.

    "Play ball, my friend. The parts I have in mind
for you Brad Pitt can't play. Now heel, Achilles,
your healing hinges on it, you dog-faced would-be
demigod. And if you don't, I'll teach
your sweet ass the meaning of 'Avenger.'

    "And so, Achilles, don't look back, my friend,
or I, your guide, will slip away from you—
Eurydice cast down and out of reach.
But tossed like plankton on the sea, absorb
the bioluminescence from within.
In time, look up and out with me. Right now,
the darkness poised below will swallow you.
One day we'll go together. Dante's plan
won't work in our chaotic times. You have
no elders, father, sage to shepherd you.
No Virgil. So a woman must extend
a hand as conduit and commissure
to lead you down on your tenebrous path,
then surge you toward a surer healing light.

    "Achilles, hope in vain that you're not cursed
to wander in and out of darkness. No man
escapes that fate. Your only balm is that
with luck from time to time your soul will prosper."